tick, tick...BOOM!

INT. THEATER - NIGHT - 1992 - VIDEO

Grainy VHS footage of a darkened stage against a bare brick
wall. JON (32) emerges from the wings, striding confidently to
a microphone stand at the lip of the stage, met by a smattering
of APPLAUSE.

                    JON
          Hi. I'm Jon. I am a musical theater
          writer, one of the last of my species.

Some LAUGHTER from the Audience. Jon frowns.

                    JON (CONT'D)
          Lately, I've been hearing this...
          sound. Everywhere I go. Like a...
          tick. Tick. Tick.

We begin to hear it with him: TICK, TICK, TICK.

                    JON (CONT'D)
          Like a time bomb in some cheesy B-
          movie or Saturday morning cartoon. The
          fuse has been lit.

The TICKING grows louder.

                    JON (CONT'D)
          The clock counts down the seconds as
          the flame gets closer, and closer, and
          closer, until all at once --

                                        SMASH TO:

INT. MOONDANCE DINER - DAY - 1990 - VHS

More grainy footage from a shaky, handheld camcorder. Jon
appears behind the counter of the diner, carrying a tray with
an elaborate breakfast spread, a flower in his mouth,
trumpeting his arrival -- making a complete idiot of himself
for the amusement of SUSAN (30), seated at the counter,
laughing, deeply in love.

Over the home video, we begin to hear her VOICE.

                    SUSAN (V.O.)
          This is Jonathan Larson's story.

She pulls the flower from his mouth and kisses him.

As we continue to hear her voice, a series of QUICK CUTS to
archival footage --

- A CROWD wrapped around the block outside New York Theatre Workshop in 1996.

                    SUSAN (V.O.)
          Before the Tony Awards.

- CLOSE ON a flyer affixed to the door of the theater: "All performances of *Rent* through the March 31 extension are SOLD OUT!"

                    SUSAN (V.O.)
          Before the Pulitzer Prize. Before...

The CUTS come faster --

- Another, larger CROWD wrapped around the block outside of the Nederlander Theatre in 1996, *Rent* emblazoned on the marquee.

- Adam Pascal and Daphne Rubin-Vega on the cover of *Newsweek*.

- On the stage of the Nederlander Theatre, ANTHONY RAPP, costumed as Mark Cohen, addresses the audience.

                    ANTHONY RAPP
          We dedicate this opening night and
          every performance to our friend,
          Jonathan Larson...

- JULIE and AL LARSON stand and applaud, overcome by emotion, at the Tony Awards.

                    SUSAN (V.O.)
          ... we lost him.

INT. MOONDANCE DINER - DAY - 1990 - VHS

Back to the diner, where Jon pops open a bottle of champagne.

                    SUSAN (V.O.)
          Everything you're about to see is
          true. Except for the parts Jonathan
          made up.

INT. THEATER - NIGHT - 1992

Jon grabs the microphone, crosses to a grand piano. He sits at the piano bench. A small BAND and two vocalists, KARESSA and ROGER (both early 30s), are arrayed behind him.

                    JON
          The date is January 26th, 1990.

NOTE: Throughout the film, we move back and forth between Jon in **1992**, performing the show, and the events he is narrating as they occur in **1990**.

INT. JON'S BEDROOM - DAY - 1990

Jon, at the keyboard, begins to find and play a CHORD PROGRESSION, out-of-time at first, slowly beginning to take shape, the CHORDS of **30/90**.

> JON (V.O.)
> The setting: the barren, unfashionable no-man's land between SoHo and Greenwich Village.

EXT. DOWNTOWN STREET - MORNING - 1990

Jon bikes down the sidewalk outside of the Moondance Diner.

INT. THEATER - NIGHT - 1992

Jon plays the same CHORD PROGRESSION on the grand piano.

> JON (V.O.)
> I have two keyboards...

INT. LIVING ROOM - CONTINUOUS - 1990

FLASH TO a boxy computer on a surprisingly well-organized desk.

> JON (V.O.)
> ...a Macintosh computer...

FLASH TO Finster perched on the sofa.

> JON (V.O.)
> ... a cat...

FLASH TO his copious music library.

> JON (V.O.)
> ... an impressive collection of compact discs, cassettes, and records of other people's music...

FLASH TO his precariously overstuffed bookshelves.

> JON (V.O.)
> ... bookshelves sagging under the weight of plays and novels I didn't write.

FLASH TO a type-written manuscript of *Superbia*.

                    JON (V.O.)
          I have an original dystopian rock
          musical that I have spent the last
          eight years of my life writing...

INT. JON'S BEDROOM - DAY - 1990

Jon sits on his bed, keyboard on his lap, completely,
unbearably stuck.

                    JON (V.O.)
          ... and rewriting.
               (a beat)
          And rewriting.

INT. THEATER - NIGHT - 1992

Back to Jon at the piano.

                    JON (V.O.)
          I have rejection letters from every
          major -- and minor -- producer,
          theater company, record label and film
          studio in existence. And in just over
          a week... I will be thirty years old.

As the CHORD PROGRESSION begins to pick up speed --

INT. LIVING ROOM - DAY - 1990

FLASH TO the cover of the *West Side Story* cast recording LP.

                    JON (V.O.)
          Older than Stephen Sondheim when he
          had his first Broadway show.

FLASH TO the cassette cover of The Beatles' *Let It Be.*

                    JON (V.O.)
          Older than Paul McCartney when he
          wrote his *last* song with John Lennon.

FLASH TO an old home movie of little JON and JULIE.

                    JON (V.O.)
          By the time my parents were thirty,
          they already had two kids. They had
          careers with steady paychecks. A
          mortgage.

INT. THEATER - NIGHT - 1992

Back to Jon at the keyboard.

                              JON
               In eight days, my youth will be over
               forever. And what exactly do I have to
               show for myself?

He STOPS playing. He takes a breath in the silence.

                              JON   (CONT'D)
               Happy Birthday.

He SLAMS his fingers back on the keys -- resuming the chord
progression, as he begins to sing.

                              JON   (CONT'D)
               STOP THE CLOCK -- TAKE TIME OUT
               TIME TO REGROUP BEFORE YOU LOSE THE
               BOUT

The Band comes in behind him, as the song picks up energy.

                              JON (CONT'D)
               FREEZE THE FRAME -- BACK IT UP
               TIME TO REFOCUS BEFORE THEY WRAP IT UP
               YEARS ARE GETTING SHORTER
               LINES ON YOUR FACE ARE GETTING LONGER
               FEEL LIKE YOU'RE TREADING WATER
               BUT THE RIPTIDE'S GETTING STRONGER
               DON'T PANIC, DON'T JUMP SHIP
               CAN'T FIGHT IT, LIKE TAXES
               AT LEAST IT HAPPENS ONLY ONCE IN YOUR
               LIFE
               THEY'RE SINGING, "HAPPY BIRTHDAY"
               YOU JUST WANNA LAY DOWN AND CRY
               NOT JUST ANOTHER BIRTHDAY, IT'S 30/90
               WHY CAN'T YOU STAY 29?
               HELL, YOU STILL FEEL LIKE YOU'RE 22
               TURN THIRTY 1990
               BANG! YOU'RE DEAD
               WHAT CAN YOU DO?
               WHAT CAN YOU DO?
               WHAT CAN YOU DO?

As the Band continues to UNDERSCORE --

INT. MOONDANCE DINER - DAY - 1990

Lunch at the diner, bustling with patrons, Jon behind the
counter. MICHAEL (30) hurries through the door.

                              MICHAEL
               I made ten copies.

He hands Jon a thick stack of photocopies, as Jon hands him a cup of coffee and a bag of take-out in exchange. Jon glances through the stack: sheet music and scripts for *Superbia*.

                    JON
          You are an angel on earth.

                    MICHAEL
          This is the last time. Seriously.

Michael reaches for his wallet. Jon shuts it down fast.

                    JON
          No, thank you. No, no, no. I got you.

                    MICHAEL
          I'm going to pay...

                    JON
          You're not going to pay. I don't want
          you to pay.

CAROLYN (33) comes by, carrying a tray full of dirty dishes, wrinkling her nose at the smell.

                    CAROLYN
          Somebody needs to take out this trash.

FREDDY (25) comes over to Michael, carrying his own tray of dirty dishes, as Jon goes to handle the trash.

                    FREDDY
          I heard you're moving out of Jon's
          place. End of an era.
                (sotto)
          We hear him sobbing in the fridge most
          mornings. It's very sad.

                    JON
                (to Carolyn)
          You're coming next Friday, right?

                    CAROLYN
                (feigning ignorance)
          What's next Friday?

Before Jon can answer --

                    MICHAEL AND FREDDY
          The *Superbia* workshop.

                    MICHAEL
          I'm surprised he hasn't mentioned it.

                    FREDDY
          It sounds vaguely familiar...

                    JON
              (defensive)
          This is the biggest break I've ever
          had. This is *that* moment. It's the
          first time people are going to see the
          show that aren't just us.

                    FREDDY
          Well, it's good that you're not
          putting too much pressure on it or
          anything...

Carolyn and Michael laugh.

                    JON
          No, but it's true, though. You get to
          a certain age and you stop being a
          writer that waits tables and you
          become... a waiter with a hobby.

                    MICHAEL
          Boo Boo. You need to ask yourself: in
          this moment, are you letting yourself
          be led by fear or by love?

As Jon considers the question, he hefts the trash bag out of
its bin. The bottom rips, sending some kind of unidentifiable
liquid all over his shoes.

INT. THEATER - NIGHT - 1992

Roger launches into the next verse of the song.

                    ROGER
          CLEAR THE RUNWAY -- MAKE ANOTHER PASS
          TRY ONE MORE APPROACH BEFORE YOU'RE
          OUT OF GAS

                    JON
          FRIENDS ARE GETTING FATTER
          HAIRS ON YOUR HEAD ARE GETTING THINNER
          FEEL LIKE A CLEAN UP BATTER
          ON A TEAM THAT AIN'T A WINNER.

                    ROGER
          DON'T FREAK OUT, DON'T STRIKE OUT
          CAN'T FIGHT IT, LIKE CITY HALL

                    JON
          AT LEAST YOU'RE NOT ALONE
          YOUR FRIENDS ARE THERE TOO

INT. JON'S APARTMENT - DAY - 1990

Matching Jon and Roger in the concert, Jon and Michael sing
together, as Jon helps stack boxes with Michael.

                    JON
          THEY'RE SINGING, "HAPPY BIRTHDAY"

          JON (CONT'D)   MICHAEL
YOU JUST WISH YOU COULD RUN   YOU JUST WISH YOU COULD RUN
AWAY   AWAY

                    JON (CONT'D)
          WHO CARES ABOUT A BIRTHDAY? BUT --

          JON (CONT'D)   MICHAEL
30/90, HEY   30/90, HEY

                    JON (CONT'D)
          CAN'T YOU BE OPTIMISTIC?

          JON (CONT'D)   MICHAEL
YOU'RE NO LONGER THE INGENUE   YOU'RE NO LONGER THE INGENUE
TURN THIRTY, 1990   TURN THIRTY, 1990

                    JON (CONT'D)
          BOOM! YOU'RE PASSÉ

          JON (CONT'D)   MICHAEL
WHAT CAN YOU DO?   WHAT CAN YOU DO?
WHAT CAN YOU DO?   OOH
WHAT CAN YOU DO?

As the Band continues to UNDERSCORE --

INT. STRAND BOOK STORE - DAY - 1990

Jon walks beside Susan through the dusty stacks, Susan staring
at him in disbelief.

                    SUSAN
          You just *quit*?

                    JON
          I didn't *quit* quit. I gave my notice.

                    SUSAN
          That's exactly -- it's the same thing.

                    JON
          No. I still have two weeks left.

Jon spies a beautiful book of expensive music manuscript paper.
He picks it up.

                         JON (CONT'D)
              I'm allowing myself to be led by love.

                         SUSAN
                    (perplexed)
              What?

                         JON
              Rosa has another client -- remember
              Craig Carnelia?

                         SUSAN
              This is Rosa, your agent who hasn't
              returned your calls in a year?

                         JON
              That's the one. She invited the entire
              theater industry to a workshop of
              Craig's musical last year. By
              intermission, some producer had
              already written him a check for ten
              thousand dollars.

                         SUSAN
              I wish you didn't have to think like
              that.

                         JON
              It's expensive to make art.

                         SUSAN
              No, it's expensive to make art *here*.

                         JON
              But worth every penny...

Susan nods to the book of manuscript paper.

                         SUSAN
              How are you going to pay for that?

Susan gently takes the book out of his hands. As Jon follows
her down the aisle, the PATRONS around them join in singing.

          JON   SUSAN AND PATRONS
PETER PAN AND TINKERBELL   AH
WHICH WAY TO NEVER NEVER LAND?   AH
EMERALD CITY'S GONE TO HELL
SINCE THE WIZARD

                    JON, SUSAN, AND PATRONS
              BLEW OFF HIS COMMAND

                         JON
               ON THE STREETS YOU HEAR THE VOICES
               LOST CHILDREN, CROCODILES
               BUT YOU'RE NOT INTO...

INT. JON'S APARTMENT - DAY - 1990 - MOS

As Michael packs up his bedroom, Jon stares at the mounting
pile of moving boxes.

                         JON (V.O.)
               MAKING CHOICES

INT. YMCA LOCKER ROOM - NIGHT - 1990 - MOS

Jon, toweling off from the pool, stares at himself in the
mirror, sucking in his gut.

                         JON (V.O.)
               WICKED WITCHES

INT. YMCA POOL - NIGHT - 1990 - MOS

Jon swims laps in the otherwise empty pool.

                         JON (V.O.)
               POPPY FIELDS OR MEN BEHIND THE CURTAIN

INT. MOONDANCE DINER - DAY- 1990 - MOS

In the BUSTLING restaurant, Jon races to grab two plates of
food from under the heat lamp.

                         JON (V.O.)
               TIGER LILIES, RUBY SLIPPERS

INT. THEATER - NIGHT - 1992

Roger and Karessa come in.

                         ALL
               CLOCK IS TICKING, THAT'S FOR CERTAIN

                         JON
               THEY'RE SINGING, "HAPPY BIRTHDAY"

          JON (CONT'D)   ROGER AND KARESSA
I JUST WISH IT ALL WERE A DREAM   HAPPY BIRTHDAY

                         JON (CONT'D)
               IT FEELS MUCH MORE LIKE DOOMSDAY
               FUCK

                          ALL
         30/90

                          JON
         SEEMS LIKE I'M IN FOR A TWISTER

             JON (CONT'D)   ROGER AND KARESSA
    I DON'T SEE A RAINBOW, DO YOU?   AH, AH

                          ALL
         TURN 30 IN THE 90S

INT. JON'S BEDROOM - NIGHT - 1990 - MOS

Jon lies in bed, wide awake, as Susan sleeps beside him.

                          JON
         INTO MY HANDS NOW
         THE BALL HAS PASSED

                                              FLASH TO:

EXT. TIMES SQUARE - NIGHT - 1990 - MOS

Jon rides his bike through seedy, neon-glistening streets.

                          JON
         I WANT THE SPOILS, BUT NOT TOO FAST

                                              FLASH TO:

EXT. ROOF - NIGHT - 1990 - MOS

Jon stands on his roof, staring out at the Hudson River.

             JON (V.O.)   ROGER AND KARESSA (V.O.)
    THE WORLD IS CALLING   AH
    IT'S NOW OR NEVERLAND   AH

                                              FLASH TO:

INT. JON'S BEDROOM - DAY - 1990

Jon pushes himself away from his computer, unable to stare at
it for a moment longer.

                          JON
         WHY CAN'T I STAY HERE FOREVER AND

                                              FLASH TO:

INT. MOONDANCE DINER - DAY - 1990 - MOS

Freddy pirouettes through the packed diner.

                         JON (V.O.)
          30/90
          30/90

                                        FLASH TO:

INT. SUBWAY - DAY - 1990 - MOS

Jon scribbles notes to himself in a small spiral notebook.

                         ROGER AND KARESSA (V.O.)
          30/90
          30/90
          30, 30/90

                                        BACK TO:

INT. THEATER - NIGHT - 1992

The song builds to a thunderous CRESCENDO.

                         JON
               WHAT CAN I DO?

                         ROGER AND KARESSA
          30/90
          30, 30/90

                         ALL
               WHAT CAN I DO?

APPLAUSE as the song ends.

                         JON
               Ladies and gentlemen, please give it
               up for our band, and for my very,
               very, very dear friends, Roger and
               Karessa, on vocals.
                    (then)
               Friday night...

INT. LIVING ROOM - EVENING - 1990

Streamers and balloons fill the apartment as Michael stands by
the answering machine, scrolling through messages, suitcase at
his feet. After a BEEP --

                         DEBORAH (V.O.)
               Hi Jonathan, it's Deborah. Susan just
               dropped off your music for tonight's
               dance recital --

Michael fast-forwards through the message, his impatience
betraying some anxiety. Deborah's voice returns.

> DEBORAH (V.O.)
> -- but I can't get the speakers to
> work --

Jon enters, grocery bags in hand. Michael stops the message.

> JON
> How was Philly?

> MICHAEL
> I went from the airport to a
> conference room and then back to the
> airport three hours later.

> JON
> That sounds amazing.

INT. THEATER - NIGHT - 1992

Jon speaks at the microphone at the front of the stage.

> JON
> Michael was an amazing actor. He was
> the lead in every play in high school,
> college. Then we moved to New York...

EXT. ROOF - NIGHT - FLASHBACK - 1988

Michael, frustrated, vents to Jon as they stand together,
passing a joint.

> MICHAEL
> I am sick of waking up at five to get
> in line outside the Equity building
> and wait all day -- praying that the
> director actually agrees to even *see*
> anyone that's non-union. And then when
> I finally do get in the room, I sing
> six measures if I'm lucky before they
> cut me off and call me the wrong name -
> - Juan, Pedro, Carlos, *lo que sea*...

INT. THEATER - NIGHT - 1992

Jon, back at the microphone.

> JON
> A week later, he got a job at a fancy
> advertising company, making high-five
> figures. Health care. Dental. He never
> looked back.

INT. LIVING ROOM - EVENING - 1990

Back to the apartment. Jon pulls some top-shelf liquor from the bags, sets it on the table beside a vase of bodega flowers.

                    MICHAEL
          You know, for someone who's broke, you
          could probably spend a little bit less
          on party planning.

                    JON
          What's the point of having money if
          you can't spend it on the people you
          love?

                    MICHAEL
               (laughing)
          Yeah, except you don't *have* any money.

                    JON
          Oh, *right*...

Michael sees a Con Edison bill on the table, picks it up.

                    MICHAEL
          This has been sitting here for a week.

                    JON
          I'm on it.

                    MICHAEL
          Yes, you seem very on it.

Michael grabs his suitcase, takes it to his room to unpack.

                    MICHAEL (CONT'D)
          Pretty soon you won't have me around
          to remind you to pay bills on time.

                    JON
               (facetious)
          How will I ever survive?

                    MICHAEL
          That's actually a very real question.
          Have you found a new roommate yet?

                    JON
          I've been a little busy. My workshop
          is next week.

                    MICHAEL
          What workshop?

Jon is about to be offended, when he realizes.

                    JON
          That was funny.

Jon reaches into his shirt pocket and pulls out his small
spiral-ring notebook and a pencil. He scribbles on a blank
page: "Fear or love?" He underlines the words. Michael calls
from the bedroom.

                    MICHAEL
          What time's the show tonight?

                    JON
          Curtain's at eight.

                    MICHAEL
          I've heard the dancing is amazing but
          the music sucks...

As we PRE-LAP a propulsive dance score --

INT. DANCE THEATER - NIGHT - 1990

Jon sits in the audience beside Michael, watching the show, an
athletic piece for eight female DANCERS, moving to the score
that Jon wrote. Jon's eyes are riveted on Susan.

                    JON (V.O.)
          Susan grew up in a small town in the
          Midwest, went to college to study
          biology. She thought she'd become a
          doctor -- maybe teach. But then she
          fell in love with modern dance instead
          -- every parents' dream, right? She
          moved to New York without knowing a
          soul. Four years later, she's already
          danced with every major choreographer
          in the city -- Paul, Trisha, Merce.

INT. THEATER - NIGHT - 1992

Jon stands with the microphone.

                    JON
          1990. This was the year she was
          finally going to join a company. Not
          just go from job to job -- actually
          have a home, an artistic family. And
          she was ready. This was her year. She
          knew it. Then she fractured her ankle
          during a dress rehearsal. Six months
          of rehab later... she's dancing again.
          It's just...
                              (MORE)

                        JON (CONT'D)
          whatever that moment was when she
          knew... all of a sudden, she doesn't
          know anymore.
               (a beat)
          Susan is a real artist. She doesn't
          care about seeing her name in the *New
          York Times*. It doesn't matter to her
          if she's dancing in front of five
          people or five thousand.

INT. DANCE THEATER - NIGHT - 1990

Seated in the audience, Jon hears the sudden sound of TICKING
underneath the SCORE.

                        JON (V.O.)
          And then there's the matter of us...

As the Dancers hit a final pose and the stage lights fade out,
Jon joins the rest of the Audience in applauding -- the
CLAPPING and CHEERS drowning out the TICKING altogether.

INT. JON'S APARTMENT - NIGHT - 1990

A raucous cast party underway, the tiny living room jam-packed
with FRIENDS. Wine and beer flow. Susan stands with Michael.

                        SUSAN
          You know he can't afford any of this,
          right?

                        MICHAEL
          Well, you know how much he loves
          making a fuss. Especially about you...

Susan smiles, something nagging at her.

INT. JON'S APARTMENT - LATER - NIGHT - 1990

Jon huddles with Freddy and Carolyn.

                        FREDDY
          After everything we've done for him,
          he walks away...

                        JON
          I'm leaving you my mix tapes. You can
          play them in remembrance of me.

Michael comes by, carrying two glasses of wine, one of which he
hands to Carolyn.

                    MICHAEL
Jonathan Larson's famous Moondance
Diner mix tapes. Who doesn't love show
tunes with their French Toast?

                    JON
Actually, it's not just show tunes.
It's a very eclectic mix.

                    CAROLYN
Someone's very touchy about the mix
tapes.

                    MICHAEL
Apparently.

                    FREDDY
I'm happy for you. I really am. I
mean, I'm also extremely bitter and
jealous and envious and hateful toward
you right now, but...
     (he smiles)
You're getting out.

                    JON
And you're going to be next.

                    FREDDY
I got a callback last week.

                    JON
That's great.

                    FREDDY
For a cruise.

                    CAROLYN
What's wrong with a cruise?

                    FREDDY
Well it's an Arctic cruise. So pretty
much everything -- every single thing
is wrong...

                    JON
How are you feeling?

Freddy takes a breath, chooses his words carefully, doesn't
want to be overly optimistic.

                    FREDDY
It's been a really good week. T-Cell
count is good. My doctor feels...
cautiously optimistic.

                         JON
          You look great.

                         FREDDY
          Oh my God, thank you, I know.

They all laugh.

INT. JON'S APARTMENT - LATER - 1990

The party has gotten louder, more packed, as Roger introduces
Jon to SCOTT (27), a banker.

                         ROGER
               (to Jon)
          Scott and I used to sing madrigals
          together in high school.

                         SCOTT
          I hated singing. I just did it for the
          pussy...

                         ROGER
          I ran into Scott in SoHo. He really,
          really wanted to come with me.

                         SCOTT
          I never get the chance to go to artist
          parties, you know? It sucks. The drugs
          there are always the best.

                         ROGER
          Scott's in finance.

                         JON
          Shocking.

                         SCOTT
          What do you do?

                         JON
          I'm the future of musical theater,
          Scott. Welcome. I'm going to grab
          another drink.

As Jon goes, Scott turns to Roger, laughs.

                         SCOTT
          That guy's hilarious.

INT. JON'S APARTMENT - LATER - 1990

The party has begun to thin out. Jon, drunker, stands with a
small group of PALS -- scattered on the sagging sofas -- giving
an impromptu performance of **BOHO DAYS**, a cappella, clapping
along to the rhythm, as he directs his audience's attention to
the various sections of the apartment.

> JON
> THIS IS THE LIFE, BO BO, BO BO BO
> THIS IS THE LIFE, BO BO, BO BO BO
> SHOWER'S IN THE KITCHEN
> THERE MIGHT BE SOME SOAP
> DISHES IN THE SINK
> BRUSH YOUR TEETH, IF YOU CAN COPE
> TOILET'S IN THE CLOSET
> YOU BETTER HOPE
> THERE'S A LIGHT BULB IN THERE

DONNA (early 30s) calls from the dark, dark bathroom.

> DONNA
> Not today!

> JON
> BO BO BO

As Jon calls out names, he points to the PEOPLE named. They
cheer for themselves.

> JON (CONT'D)
> REVOLVING DOOR ROOMMATES
> PRICK UP YOUR EARS
> FOURTEEN PEOPLE IN JUST FOUR YEARS
> ANN AND MAX AND JONATHAN
> AND CAROLYN AND KERRI
> DAVID, TIM -- NO TIM WAS JUST A GUEST
> FROM JUNE TO JANUARY

> MICHAEL
> (laughs)
> I remember Tim...

> JON
> MARGARET, LISA, DAVID, SUSIE,
> STEPHEN, JOE AND SAM
> AND ELSA, THE BILL COLLECTOR'S DREAM
> WHO IS STILL ON THE LAM
> DON'T FORGET THE NEIGHBORS
> MICHELLE AND GAY

MICHELLE and GAY (middle-aged artists) take a little bow.

                         JON (CONT'D)
          MORE LIKE A FAMILY
          THAN A FAMILY, HEY
          THE TIME IS FLYING
          AND EVERYTHING IS DYING
          I THOUGHT BY NOW
          I'D HAVE A DOG, A KID, AND WIFE
          THE SHIP IS SORT OF SINKING
          SO LET'S START DRINKING
          BEFORE WE START THINKING
          IS THIS A LIFE?
          THIS IS THE LIFE, BO BO, BO BO BO

Roger joins in harmony.

                         JON & ROGER
          THIS IS THE LIFE, BO BO, BO BO BO

The room JOINS in.

                         ALL
          THIS IS THE LIFE, BO BO, BO BO BO
          BOHEMIA

                         JON
          BOHEMIA!

CHEERS and WHISTLES erupt.

                         SCOTT
          That was freaking *amazing*. *Whoooo!*

EXT. ROOF - MINUTES LATER - 1990

Susan stands on the roof, lost in thought, staring at the
water, wearing a coat. Jon comes out to find her.

                         JON
          Hey. Everyone's leaving.

                         SUSAN
          I just needed some fresh air.

                         JON
          It's freezing up here.

                         SUSAN
          Where's your coat?

                         JON
          Somewhere at the bottom of a very
          large pile.

Jon looks out toward the flickering lights on the water.

                    JON (CONT'D)
Pretty.

                    SUSAN
That's the prison barge.

                    JON
          (laughs, remembering)
Right...

                    SUSAN
You know, I heard Jacob's Pillow is
hiring new teachers for their dance
school...

                    JON
Oh yeah?

                    SUSAN
You work a couple hours a week and
then the rest of the time is yours.
Free studio space whenever you want.

                    JON
Hey, can we talk about how amazing you
were tonight?

                    SUSAN
Thank you.

                    JON
No, but truly, though.

                    SUSAN
I was thinking of maybe applying. To
the Jacob's Pillow job.
          (off his confusion)
We went last summer, remember? We saw
the new Mark Morris...

                    JON
The place in the Berkshires? You're
going to move to the Berkshires?

                    SUSAN
And not have to work thirty hours a
week doing word processing to pay the
rent? Why not? I might actually be
able to get back in shape...

                    JON
Okay. Great. Yeah. All right. Let's do
it. Let's move.

                    SUSAN
          I'm being serious.

                    JON
          Hey, *I'm* being serious. We can live in
          a log cabin and gather acorns, hunt
          squirrels...

                    SUSAN
          What are you even talking about?
          It's the Berkshires. People have
          vacation houses there. You've *been*
          there.

                    JON
               (they laugh)
          Can we go inside now? I'm just, I'm
          sorry, I'm scared I'm beginning to
          lose sensation in my extremities.

Susan laughs, takes off her coat, revealing the green velvet
dress she's wearing underneath.

                    SUSAN
          You are such a baby. Take this.

As Susan hands him the coat, he stops as he notices the dress.

                    JON
          Hold on.

                    SUSAN
               (feigns nonchalance)
          Oh. You like it?

                    SUSAN (CONT'D)
          I thought you were in such a hurry to
          get back...

INT. JON'S BEDROOM - MINUTES LATER - 1990

Jon slams on his clock radio and an R&B rendition of **GREEN
GREEN DRESS** begins to play, as he and Susan fall into bed
together, clothes beginning to come off.

INT. LIVING ROOM - CONTINUOUS - 1990

Michael, in the room next door, hears them through the thin
walls, throws on a pair of headphones, tries to drown it out.

INT. JON'S BEDROOM - CONTINUOUS - 1990

Jon and Susan entwined in bed, Jon sliding the green, green
dress off.

                         SUSAN
          That job in the Berkshires?

                         JON
                    (distracted)
          It sounds amazing...

                         SUSAN
          I already applied for it.

                         JON
          Oh yeah?

                         SUSAN
          I got it.

Now he's paying attention.

                         SUSAN (CONT'D)
          It doesn't start until June.

                         JON
          Oh. So it's just for the summer?

                         SUSAN
          It's permanent.

He stares at her, agog.

                         SUSAN (CONT'D)
          Jon?

INT./EXT. MICHAEL'S BMW - DAY - 1990

Michael drives Jon in his BMW through traffic.

                         MICHAEL
          Whoa. The Berkshires. That is... very
          far from Midtown.

                         JON
          Why is she doing this now? And she
          wants me to come with her...

                         MICHAEL
          What did you say?

                         JON
          I said: "Oh." What was I supposed to
          say? I didn't know *what* to say. I
          mean, I can't leave New York...

                         MICHAEL
          Tell her to move in with you.

                         JON
              Move in where?

                         MICHAEL
              You need a new roommate right? Two
              birds, one stone. You're welcome.

Jon changes the subject.

                         JON
              What happened to that guy you were
              seeing? David? I thought you guys were
              great together.

Michael shrugs, pretending indifference.

                         MICHAEL
              It didn't work out.
                   (moving on)
              There's a focus group at the office
              this week, looking for a few more
              people. How about I sign you up?

                         JON
              So you can lure me to the dark side...

                         MICHAEL
              So I can introduce you to my
              colleagues and show them how brilliant
              you are.

                         JON
              I don't want a job in advertising.

                         MICHAEL
              I don't want you to have a job in
              advertising. But jingle-writing...

Jon is about to object, but Michael barrels over him.

                         MICHAEL (CONT'D)
              You come up with jingles all the time
              for fun, Jon. You make up songs about
              the cereal we're eating. You could get
              paid for those.

                         JON
              When *Superbia* gets produced, I'll get
              paid for my music anyway.

                         MICHAEL
                   (ncds, equivocal)
              That's true...

They pull into the courtyard of a luxury condo building.

                    MICHAEL (CONT'D)
          And we are here. Home, sweet home.

Jon stares out the window at the gleaming glass high-rise.

INT. THEATER - NIGHT - 1992

Jon speaks into the microphone.

                    JON
          Oh. My. God.

EXT. VICTORY TOWERS - DAY - 1990

Jon steps out, taking in the marble fountain in the center of
the courtyard, as the MUSICAL INTRO to **NO MORE** begins.

                    JON (V.O.)
          Michael tosses the keys to the parking
          attendant -- what apartment building
          has a *parking attendant*?

Michael hands Jon a moving box from the back seat, grabs
another one, and shuts the door. As Jon follows him through the
glass revolving doors...

INT. VICTORY TOWERS LOBBY - CONTINUOUS - 1990

A white lobby, austere like an art gallery. A heavy-set,
mustachioed DOORMAN (40s) nods from his desk, as Michael leads
Jon toward the elevators.

                    JON (V.O.)
          Fresh flowers in the lobby. An old
          white lady with a tiny dog. Is this
          real life?

EXT. GREENWICH STREET - NIGHT - 1990

Michael and Jon trudge through snow, hefting massive sacks of
laundry, as Michael sings to him.

                    MICHAEL
               NO MORE
               WALKING THIRTEEN BLOCKS
               WITH THIRTY POUNDS OF LAUNDRY
               IN THE FREEZING DEAD OF WINTER

INT. JON'S APARTMENT - STAIRWELL - NIGHT - 1990

Laundry bags in hand, Jon schleps up the grimy, uneven steps
behind Michael.

                    MICHAEL
          NO MORE
          WALKING UP SIX FLIGHTS OF STAIRS
          OR THROWING DOWN THE KEY
          BECAUSE THERE IS NO BUZZER

Michael gestures to exposed wires dangling from the ceiling.

                    MICHAEL (CONT'D)
          NO MORE FAULTY WIRING
          NO MORE CROOKED FLOORS
          NO MORE SPITTING OUT MY ULTRA BRITE
          ON TOP OF DIRTY DISHES
          IN THE ONE AND ONLY SINK

As they reach their apartment, Michael turns the key and pushes
open the door to --

INT. MICHAEL'S APARTMENT - DAY - 1990

Michael leads Jon into his gleaming new apartment.

                    MICHAEL
          HELLO TO MY WALK IN CLOSETS
          TIDY AS PARK AVENUE
          HELLO, MY BUTCHER BLOCK TABLE
          I COULD GET USED -- I COULD GET USED
          I COULD GET USED TO YOU

INT. JON'S APARTMENT - NIGHT - 1990

Michael and Jon inspect a SLEEPING STRANGER (20s), a man passed
out on the floor of their apartment.

                    MICHAEL
          NO MORE
          CLIMBING OVER SLEEPING PEOPLE
          BEFORE YOU GET OUT THE DOOR OF YOUR
          OWN BUILDING

Michael and Jon share a look -- do you know who that is?
Neither has any idea.

Michael and Jon plop down on chairs in the living room, staring
nervously at the glowing, unvented gas wall heater.

          MICHAEL (CONT'D)   JON
NO MORE   NO MORE

                    MICHAEL (CONT'D)
          NOXIOUS FUMES FROM GAS HEATERS THAT
          ARE ILLEGAL

                         JON
          OR WILL BLOW UP WHILE YOU ARE SLEEPING

                       MICHAEL
          NO MORE

They look up to see water dripping from the discolored ceiling.

                         JON
          LEAKY CEILING

                       MICHAEL
          NO MORE

They look down to see a disconcerting aperture in the floor.

                         JON
          HOLES IN THE FLOOR

                    MICHAEL AND JON
          NO MORE

INT. JON'S APARTMENT - KITCHEN - NIGHT - 1990

Jon and Michael take in the claw-foot tub in the kitchen.

                         JON
          TAKING A SHOWER IN THE KITCHEN
          WHILE YOUR ROOMMATE'S EATING BREAKFAST

Michael and Jon stand in the tub together.

                    MICHAEL AND JON
          AND YOU'RE GETTING WATER ON HIS
          CORNFLAKES

They pull the shower curtain closed.

INT. MICHAEL'S APARTMENT - LIVING ROOM - DAY - 1990

They walk across the immaculate floors to the kitchen.

                    MICHAEL AND JON
          HELLO, TO SHINY NEW PARQUET WOOD
          FLOORS
          AS WAXED AS A WEALTHY GIRL'S LEGS
          HELLO, DEAR MISTER DISHWASHER

                       MICHAEL
          I COULD GET USED

                         JON
          I COULD GET USED

                         MICHAEL
               I COULD GET USED

                          JON
               I COULD GET USED

                    MICHAEL AND JON
               I COULD GET USED TO YOU

INT. JON'S APARTMENT - NIGHT - 1990

Jon pops open the fridge. An unidentifiable, mold-covered piece
of once-food sits on the shelf.

                          JON
               NO MORE EXOTIC

Michael slides the dead bolt into place on the door, as SIRENS
sound from outside the apartment.

                       MICHAEL
               NO MORE NEUROTIC

                    MICHAEL AND JON
               NO MORE ANYTHING
               BUT PLEASANTLY ROBOTIC

INT. MICHAEL'S APARTMENT - LIVING ROOM - DAY

Michael flips a switch and all of the blinds in the apartment
open at once, letting in a burst of mid-day sunshine.

                       MICHAEL
               WE'RE MOVING ON UP

                          JON
               WE'RE MOVING ON UP

                       MICHAEL
               TO THE EAST SIDE

                          JON
               TO THE EAST SIDE

                    MICHAEL AND JON
               TO A DELUXE APARTMENT IN THE SKY

INT. VICTORY TOWERS LOBBY - DAY - 1990

Fully immersed in the fantasy, Michael and Jon, in tuxedos,
stroll in, Michael handing the Doorman a $20 bill with a wink.

                    MICHAEL AND JON
          HELLO, TO DEAR MISTER DOORMAN
          WHO LOOKS LIKE CAPTAIN KANGAROO
          HELLO DEAR FELLOW, AND HOW DO YOU DO?

A full party is underway in the lobby -- beautiful PEOPLE,
SUPERMODELS male and female, dancing.

                       MICHAEL
              I COULD GET USED

                        JON
              I COULD GET USED

                       MICHAEL
          EVEN SEDUCED

                        JON
          EVEN SEDUCED

                    MICHAEL AND JON
          I COULD GET USED TO YOU, OH --

The beautiful people follow Michael and Jon to the elevator.

INT. VICTORY TOWERS - ELEVATORS - DAY - 1990

Michael and Jon stand in the packed elevator, surrounded by the
beautiful people.

                       MICHAEL
              -- I COULD GET USED

                        JON
              I COULD GET USED

                       MICHAEL
          EVEN SEDUCED

                        JON
          EVEN SEDUCED

                    MICHAEL AND JON
          I COULD GET USED TO YOU

As the elevator doors shut with a DING --

                                        MATCH CUT TO:

INT. SUBWAY - DAY - 1990

Jon stands in the same position, jammed into a PACKED subway
car. He watches as the subway doors, sliding shut, are stopped
by a would-be PASSENGER trying to squeeze onto the train.

                              ANNOUNCER (V.O.)
                    Stand clear of the closing doors or
                    we're not going anywhere. I swear to
                    God. I'm talking to you in the back.

                              IRA (PRE-LAP)
                    You still don't have the song...

INT. MOONDANCE DINER - MINUTES LATER - 1990

Jon sits at a table across from IRA WEITZMAN, cups of coffee
and a script of *Superbia* between them.

                              JON
                    This has never happened to me before.
                    I usually write a song in a day. Last
                    week, I wrote a song about sugar in
                    three hours.

                              IRA
                         (puzzled)
                    A song about sugar?

Jon sings a bit of **SUGAR** a cappella.

                              JON
                    SUGAR, SHE'S REFINED
                    FOR A SMALL PRICE
                    SHE BLOWS MY MIND

                              IRA
                    Why would you do that?

                              JON
                    It was an exercise.

                              IRA
                    In what?

                              JON
                    I like to see if I can write a song
                    about anything.

                              IRA
                    Why don't you try to see if you can
                    write a song for your musical that's
                    being presented to an audience in six
                    days instead?

INT. THEATER - NIGHT - 1992

Back to Jon on stage.

                    JON
          Ira Weitzman. Head of Musical Theater
          at Playwrights Horizons. The first
          and, so far, *only* actual theater
          person to offer to put on a workshop
          of *Superbia*.

INT. MOONDANCE DINER - DAY - 1990

Back to Jon and Ira at the Diner.

                    JON
          I'm starting to think that maybe I
          don't need it...

                    IRA
          You do.

                    JON
          You know, you're the only person who's
          ever said that. Just so you know.

                    IRA
          You're telling me, in the five years
          you've been writing this musical --

INT. THEATER - NIGHT - 1992

Jon stands at the lip of the stage.

                    JON
          Eight years, actually.

INT. LIFE CAFE - DAY - 1990

The scene RESUMES where it stopped, Ira in mid-sentence.

                    IRA
          -- no one else has told you that
          you're missing a song for Elizabeth in
          the second act?

                    JON
          No.

                    JON (V.O.)
          Okay. I'm lying.

INT. THEATER - NIGHT - 1992

Back to Jon with the mic at the front of the stage.

                    JON
          One person did say that.
               (then)
          For years, I was part of this musical
          theater writing workshop...

INT. REHEARSAL STUDIO - NIGHT - 1988

A dozen aspiring musical WRITERS sit in rows of folding chairs,
as Jon sits at a piano and sings a section of **LCD READOUT**.

                    JON
          LIQUID CRYSTAL DIGITAL READOUT
          FLOATING ON A SEA OF GRAY
          HELP ME FALL ASLEEP
          I'M TIRED
          IT'S NEARLY THE BREAK OF DAY

                    JON (V.O.)
          Once a week, we would gather -- the
          few surviving members of our dwindling
          tribe -- to watch one of us present
          what we were working on to a panel of,
          well, real writers...

                    JON
          LIQUID CRYSTAL DIGITAL READOUT
          DIVIDING THE DAY AWAY

                    JON (V.O.)
          The theater legends who'd created the
          Broadway shows we'd grown up dragging
          our parents into the city to see.

                    JON
          COUNTING SLOWLY, MEASURING MOMENTS
          IF YOU COULD TALK, WHAT WOULD YOU SAY?

Seated on the other side of the room, we PAN slowly over WALTER
BLOOM (50s), a successful musical theater writer, stone-faced,
watching Jon perform.

                    JON (V.O.)
          The panel would change every week. The
          night I presented, people began to
          buzz as soon as we walked through the
          door -- "Is it really him?" It was.

PANNING past Bloom, we LAND on STEPHEN SONDHEIM (58).

                    JON (V.O.)
          Stephen. Sondheim.

INT. REHEARSAL STUDIO - LATER - 1988

Four folding chairs are now arranged at the front of the room.
Jon sits, on display, listening to Bloom critique his work.

                    WALTER BLOOM
          Okay. I'll start: I'm lost. I don't
          know what the show is. Is it social
          commentary? Is it science fiction? And
          the music... it's the same thing. Is
          it rock? Is it Broadway? Is it both?
          Neither?
               (turns to Sondheim)
          Steve? What do you think?

                    SONDHEIM
          I have to say, I disagree pretty
          strongly, Walter. I think this is a
          musical that knows exactly what it is.

                    WALTER BLOOM
          Yes. Of course. Yes. Absolutely.

                    SONDHEIM
               (to Jon)
          The world you've created is really
          original. It's fascinating. The
          problem is that it's not terribly easy
          to follow the emotional thread. The
          details distract us from connecting
          with the characters. Does that make
          sense?

Walter nods, as though this is what he said, too.

                    WALTER BLOOM
          Yes, we're on the same page here.
          That's exactly how I felt. We're
          saying the same thing. Just
          differently. But the music... I'm
          sorry, the music just wasn't there.

                    SONDHEIM
          I actually thought the songs were
          swell.

                    WALTER BLOOM
          As did I. The individual songs.

                    SONDHEIM
          I particularly liked the one the young
          man sings at the end of the first act.
          First-rate lyric. And tune.

The aspiring composers in the room share stupefied glances.

                    JON (V.O.)
          "First-rate lyric. And tune."

INT. THEATER - NIGHT - 1992

Jon beams at the audience.

                    JON
          Those five words were enough to keep
          me going for the next two years.

                    SONDHEIM (PRE-LAP)
          You're missing a song.

INT. REHEARSAL STUDIO - LATER - NIGHT - 1988

At the end of class, the other writers finish clearing out, as
Jon packs up his things. Sondheim approaches.

                    SONDHEIM
               (forgetting the name)
          For the young woman...

                    JON
          Elizabeth.

                    SONDHEIM
          Elizabeth. It's the turning point of
          the show. Your protagonist is either
          going in this direction or that
          direction. Somebody needs to wake him
          up, shake some sense into him.

                    WALTER BLOOM
          You know, it's funny.

We WIDEN to find Walter, seated, listening in on the
conversation.

                    WALTER
          I was going to say the exact same
          thing.

                    JON (PRE-LAP)
          Can we talk about musicians?

INT. MOONDANCE DINER - DAY - 1990

Back to the Diner, as Ira frowns, not sure what he means.

                         JON
          Because if it's only four, I need to
          figure out how to divide the bass
          parts --

                         IRA
          Jon. This is a reading. You'll have a
          piano.

                         JON
          I wrote a rock score. At the very
          least, I need drums, a synth, guitar --

                         IRA
          A great song should sound great
          without *any* instruments.

                         JON
          You're right. Let's do it a cappella.
          Or, you know what? Let's just skip the
          songs. We can get the audience in and
          out in half an hour.

Ira sighs -- things always escalate the same way with Jon.

                         IRA
          I will look at the budget and try to
          dig up money for another musician.

                         JON
          Two more *and* piano is the absolute
          bare minimum for this.

                         IRA
          Have you spoken to Rosa?

As Jon takes in the question --

                                                      FLASH TO:

INT. JON'S APARTMENT - NIGHT - FLASHBACK - 1990

Jon paces, on the phone.

                         JON
          Hey Rosa. This is Jonathan Larson,
          your client. I've left multiple
          messages with your secretary --

INT. MOONDANCE DINER - DAY - 1990

Back to the Diner.

                    IRA
          Rosa Stevens is still your agent,
          right?

                    JON
          Oh yeah, no, we talk constantly.

                    IRA
          Has she sent out invites for the
          presentation yet? We haven't gotten a
          lot of RSVPs.

Jon's stomach sinks.

                    IRA (CONT'D)
          It's fine. Nobody has more contacts in
          the industry than Rosa. I'm sure
          she'll get some good people there for
          you...
                    (stands to go)
          I'll see you Monday. First day of
          rehearsal. And finish the song
          already, please...

INT. JON'S APARTMENT - NIGHT - 1990 - MONTAGE

- Jon stares at his computer screen. On it, a completely blank
Word document titled: "New Song."

- Jon stands in the kitchen, on the telephone.

                    JON (ON PHONE)
          I'm calling to leave a message for Mr.
          Sondheim. This is Jonathan Larson.

- Jon sits in front of the television -- Jesse Helms on the
evening news. He takes out his pad from his shirt pocket,
writes: "The boss is wrong as rain."

- Another phone call in the kitchen.

                    JON (ON PHONE) (CONT'D)
          Hi there, this is a message for Joe
          Papp.

- Another phone call in the kitchen.

                    JON (ON PHONE) (CONT'D)
          Bernie Gersten.

- Another phone call.

                      JON (ON PHONE) (CONT'D)
The artistic director of the Shubert
Organization.

- Another phone call.

                      JON (ON PHONE) (CONT'D)
La MaMa.

- Another phone call.

                      JON (ON PHONE) (CONT'D)
Larson. L-A-R-S-O-N.

- Another phone call.

                      JON (ON PHONE) (CONT'D)
No, not Parson.

- Another call.

                      JON (ON PHONE) (CONT'D)
It's something that's never been done
before --

- Another call.

                      JON (ON PHONE) (CONT'D)
It's going to be quite the event.

- Another call.

                      JON (ON PHONE) (CONT'D)
It has tremendous commercial
possibility.

- Another call.

                      JON (ON PHONE) (CONT'D)
We're filling up fast, so I just
wanted to make sure you got your spot.

- Another call.

                      JON (ON PHONE) (CONT'D)
I know that his time is limited...

- Another call.

                      JON (ON PHONE) (CONT'D)
It would be such a treat...

- Another call.

>   JON (ON PHONE) (CONT'D)
>   Zero pressure.

- Another call.

>   JON (ON PHONE) (CONT'D)
>   So can I count you in?

- Another call.

>   JON (ON PHONE) (CONT'D)
>   There will be a seat reserved for him.

- Another call.

>   JON (ON PHONE) (CONT'D)
>   *Superbia* at Playwrights Horizons.
>   10am.

- Another call.

>   JON (ON PHONE) (CONT'D)
>   Friday at 10am.

- Another call.

>   JON (ON PHONE) (CONT'D)
>   I'm so excited about Friday.

- Another call.

>   JON (ON PHONE) (CONT'D)
>   I wouldn't want you to miss it.

- Another call.

>   JON (ON PHONE) (CONT'D)
>   That's all the information I can give
>   you.

- He sits in the living room, staring at the still very much blank document on the screen.

- Jon watches a VHS copy of *Sunday In The Park With George* with Mandy Patinkin and Bernadette Peters, taped from PBS, Michael next to him, Susan lying on his shoulder, watching.

>   MICHAEL
>   They should put every Sondheim musical
>   on PBS.

>   JON
>   *Sunday*'s a pretty good start...

                    MICHAEL
          I don't understand why he can't just
          tell her he loves her. Why can't he be
          an artist and love her?

                    JON
          He does love her.

                    MICHAEL
          Yeah but he can't express it.

                    JON
          Well, that's his problem.

                    MICHAEL
          Men.
               (marvels)
          Bernadette in that corset, though.

Jon stares at the screen, astonished by the stagecraft.

                    JON
          How'd he do that?

- Jon goes through the mail -- bills and more bills (a few
marked POST-DUE) and a Victoria's Secret catalogue.

                    MICHAEL
          Did you crack it yet?

                    JON
          I'm getting very close.

                    MICHAEL
          Call me if you need inspiration.

                    JON
          No. Don't go. Hang out. You can sleep
          in your old room.

                    MICHAEL
          Write the song, Boo Boo.

- Jon, at the keyboard. Susan comes to kiss him goodnight.

                    SUSAN
          They want my answer by Wednesday. On
          the job? So if we could maybe talk
          about it before then...

                    JON
          Can we talk about it tomorrow? I just
          really need to finish this song. Okay?

                    SUSAN
          Sure.

                    JON
          Are you sure you're sure?

                    SUSAN
          I'm sure.

                    JON
          You don't seem sure...

                    SUSAN
          Goodnight, Jonathan.

- Jon stares at the computer screen. On the "New Song"
document, he's written "You're" and that's it. He changes it to
"Your." He looks at it. He changes it back to "You're." He
looks at it.

INT. THEATER - NIGHT - 1992

The instrumental introduction of **JOHNNY CAN'T DECIDE** begins.
Jon sits at the piano, begins to sing.

                    JON
          BREAK OF DAY, THE DAWN IS HERE

INT. LIVING ROOM - DAWN - 1990

Jon sits at the computer, head in his hands, the sun just
beginning to rise in the window.

                    JON (V.O.)
          JOHNNY'S UP AND PACING
          COMPROMISE, OR PERSEVERE?
          HIS MIND IS RACING

INT. THEATER - NIGHT - 1992

Jon sings from the piano.

                    JON
          JOHNNY HAS NO GUIDE - JOHNNY WANTS TO
          HIDE
          CAN HE MAKE A MARK, IF HE GIVES UP HIS
          SPARK?
          JOHNNY CAN'T DECIDE

EXT. CITY STREET - DAY - 1990

Susan dances against a graffiti-tagged wall, as Jon watches,
beaming.

                    JON (V.O.)
        SUSAN LONGS TO LIVE BY THE SEA,
        SHE'S THROUGH WITH COMPETITION
        SUSAN WANTS A LIFE WITH ME
        JOHNNY'S GOT A TOUGH DECISION

INT. THEATER - NIGHT - 1992

Jon sings from the piano.

                    JON
        JOHNNY HAS NO GUIDE

Karessa joins.

                    JON AND KARESSA
        JOHNNY WANTS TO HIDE
        CAN HE SETTLE DOWN -- AND STILL NOT
        DROWN?

                    JON
        DROWN

                    JON AND KARESSA
        JOHNNY CAN'T DECIDE

INT. MICHAEL'S OFFICE - DAY - 1990

Michael sits alone at his desk, phone to his ear, the
consternation on his face belying the lyrics.

                    JON (V.O.)
        MICHAEL'S GONNA HAVE IT ALL
        HIS LUCK WILL NEVER END

INT. THEATER - NIGHT - 1992

Jon sings from the piano.

                    JON
        JOHNNY'S BACKED AGAINST THE WALL
        CAN HE BEND HIS DREAMS JUST LIKE HIS
        FRIEND?

INT. JON'S APARTMENT - DAY - 1990

Jon sits at the kitchen table, looking enviously at the
listings in the Theater section of the *Times*.

                    JON (V.O.)
        JOHNNY SEES THAT SUSAN'S RIGHT

                    JON AND KARESSA (V.O.)
        AMBITION EATS RIGHT THROUGH YOU

INT. THEATER - NIGHT - 1992

Roger joins back-up vocals.

                    JON AND ROGER
          MICHAEL DOESN'T SEE WHY JOHNNY
          HOLDS ON TIGHT
          TO THE THINGS THAT

                    ALL
          JOHNNY FEELS ARE TRUE

EXT. JON'S APARTMENT BUILDING - DAY - 1990

Jon unlocks his bike from a street sign.

                    ROGER AND KARESSA (V.O.)
          JOHNNY HAS NO GUIDE
          JOHNNY HAS NO GUIDE

Jon rides away.

INT. THEATER - NIGHT - 1992

All three sing.

                    ALL (V.O.)
          HOW CAN YOU SOAR
          IF YOU'RE NAILED TO THE
          FLOOR?

EXT. DOWNTOWN STREET - DAY - 1990

Jon rides past Duarte Square Park. He stops at a red light,
peers in.

                    ALL (V.O.)
          JOHNNY CAN'T DECIDE
          JOHNNY HAS NO GUIDE
          JOHNNY HAS NO GUIDE
          JOHNNY WANTS TO HIDE
          JOHNNY WANTS TO HIDE
          HOW DO YOU KNOW WHEN IT'S TIME TO LET
          GO?

Jon's eyes land on some ACT UP posters wheat-pasted on a
plywood construction barrier: "Silence = Death." He takes out
his spiral notebook, writes: "Why does it take a disaster for
anything to change?"

INT. THEATER - NIGHT - 1992

The song becomes a round between the three vocalists.

                              ALL
                    JOHNNY CAN'T DECIDE
                    JOHNNY CAN'T DECIDE
                    JOHNNY CAN'T DECIDE
                    DECIDE, DECIDE, DECIDE, DECIDE

Jon leans toward the microphone, takes a breath --

EXT. DOWNTOWN STREET - DAY - 1990

Jon locks his bike to a street sign outside the Moondance
Diner. He looks up, sees his own reflection in the glass door
of the restaurant.

INT. THEATER - NIGHT - 1992

The MUSIC cuts out. Jon sings alone, a cappella.

                         JON
                    JOHNNY CAN'T DECIDE

                         CAROLYN (PRE-LAP)
                    Freddy is in the emergency room.

INT. MOONDANCE DINER - DAY - 1990

A handful of early bird customers eat breakfast. Behind the
counter, Carolyn talks quietly to Jon, stressed, anxious.

                         JON
               What?

                         CAROLYN
               He woke up Saturday with a fever. He
               couldn't stop shivering...

                         JON
               He told me last week his T-cell count -
               - the doctors said it was exactly
               where they wanted it to be.

                         CAROLYN
               I guess it changed.

They sit there, taking this in, understanding what it means.

                         JON
               Shit.

A long beat.

                         JON (CONT'D)
               He's going to be fine.

                         CAROLYN
            Yeah.

                         JON
            I mean, you know how stubborn he is.
            He's a pain in the ass.

                         CAROLYN
            You're right.

                         JON
            Frankly? We should be pissed at him.
            For leaving us understaffed at Sunday
            brunch.

                         CAROLYN
            Right?

They both try to smile at this.

INT. THEATER - NIGHT - 1992

Jon sits at the piano, speaking his inner monologue.

                         JON
            Freddy -- shit. I should go to the
            hospital. When am I going to go to the
            hospital? I need to write. I need to
            talk to Susan. I need to see Freddy. I
            should call Susan.

INT. MOONDANCE DINER - DAY - 1990

Jon stands at the counter, thoughts tumbling through his mind.

                         JON (V.O.)
            Why can't I write this song? How can
            you possibly think about your show
            when your friend is in the hospital?
            What am I doing here? I need to leave,
            I need to turn around, walk out the
            door and *go*.

Just as the bell on the door RINGS as a CUSTOMER enters --

INT. THEATER - NIGHT - 1992

Jon hits a high-pitched piano key.

                         JON
            But it's 9:30 on a Sunday morning at
            the Moondance Diner. I'm not going
            anywhere.

INT. MOONDANCE DINER - DAY - 1990

The madness of Sunday brunch in full bloom. The diner is now PACKED, with a line of PATRONS waiting at the door, and the PHONE behind the counter RINGING and RINGING. A SERIES OF QUICK SCENES --

- Jon takes down an order at a two-top.

                    PATRON #1
          Do you have that wonderful Jewish
          bread?

                    PATRON #2
          Holly bread, dear. They call it holly
          bread.

- PHIL, a sweating cook, yells at Jon over the din.

                    PHIL
          Someone needs to pick up those goddamn
          eggs...

- Jon reads a name from a pad to Patrons waiting at the door.

                    JON
          Harrington.
            (a beat)
          Is there a Harrington?

- Jon finally picks up the RINGING telephone.

                    JON (CONT'D)
          Moondance, what do you want?
            (then)
          That was a Ghostbusters reference.
            (a beat)
          Do we take reservations? No, we do not
          take reservations. We're a diner.

- Carolyn races into the kitchen, searching for the right plate under the hot lights.

                    CAROLYN
          Where's my rye bread?

- An agonizingly slow-talking older man, RICHARD (70s, hard of hearing), talks to Jon, who jots down his information on a pad.

                    JON
          Name please?

                    RICHARD
          Richard.

                    JON
          For how many?

                    RICHARD
          Caplan.

                    JON
          How many in your party?

                    RICHARD
          With a C. "C" as in "cat."

                    JON
          How many in your party -- ?

                    RICHARD
          It's not a math test.

INT. THEATER - NIGHT - 1992

Jon sits at the piano, his arm poised in the air to conduct the
rest of the band.

                    JON
               ORDER.

He conducts the KEYBOARDIST, who plays a series of notes.

INT. MOONDANCE DINER - DAY - 1990

As Jon sets down his plate, a belligerent lawyer, JEREMY (40s),
looks at it disgustedly, then up at Jon.

                    JON
          Thank you for your patience.

                    JEREMY
          I said an omelet with *no yolks*. This
          is why you're just a waiter.

INT. THEATER - NIGHT - 1992

Jon once more conducts the Keyboardist.

                    JON
               TENSION.

INT. MOONDANCE DINER - DAY - 1992

Carolyn, carrying a huge tray of plates, hurries out of the
kitchen as a BUSBOY hurries in.

                              CAROLYN
              Major vomit situation in the Ladies
              Room.

Two already DRUNK WOMEN (30s) at the bar call over to Jon.

                         DRUNK WOMAN #1
              Can we get two more mimosas please?

                         DRUNK WOMAN #2
              She got a new job. So you need to put
              some Baileys in this coffee or some
              vodka in this orange juice...

                         DRUNK WOMAN #1
              Something...

INT. THEATER - NIGHT - 1992

Jon conducts.

                              JON
                    BALANCE.

The Keyboardist plays a new series of notes.

INT. MOONDANCE DINER - DAY - 1990

Jon tallies up a check at the register, the clamor around him
unbearable, as the PHONE keeps RINGING and RINGING and
RINGING...

INT. THEATER - NIGHT - 1992

Jon raises his arms to conduct the band. An intake of breath --

                              JON
                    Brunch.

INT. MOONDANCE DINER - DAY - 1990

Everything suddenly FREEZES, except for Jon, who looks upon the
scene coolly, with a certain aesthetic distance, as though
gazing upon a blank canvas.

Carolyn, the Bus Boy, and Patrons, though frozen in place, all
join him in a hushed, reverent tone, singing **SUNDAY.** Jon moves
through the diner, observing the still scene.

                              ALL
                    SUNDAY
                    IN THE BLUE, SILVER CHROMIUM DINER
                    ON THE GREEN, PURPLE, YELLOW, RED
                    STOOLS

                    JON
          SIT THE FOOLS
          WHO SHOULD EAT AT HOME
          INSTEAD, THEY PAY ON

                    ALL
          SUNDAY

Jon continues to move through the diner, sculpting each person
he passes into a pose, gradually forming a tableau vivant a la
Seurat's pointillist masterpiece, *A Sunday Afternoon on the
Island of La Grand Jette*. They are compliant clay in his hands.

                    ALL (CONT'D)
          FOR A COOL ORANGE JUICE OR A BAGEL
          ON THE SOFT, GREEN CYLINDRICAL STOOLS

                    JON
          SIT THE FOOLS
          DRINKING CINNAMON COFFEE
          OR DECAFFEINATED TEA

                    ALL
          FOREVER

The front wall of the diner slowly comes down.

                    ALL (CONT'D)
          IN THE BLUE, SILVER CHROMIUM DINER
          DRIPS THE GREEN, ORANGE, VIOLET DROOL
          FROM THE FOOLS
          WHO'D PAY LESS AT HOME
          DRINKING COFFEE
          LIGHT
          AND DARK

                    JON AND PHIL
          AND CHOLESTEROL

                    JON
          AND BUMS, BUMS, BUMS, BUMS, BUMS,
          BUMS, BUMS, BUMS, BUMS, BUMS

An ensemble of HOMELESS PEOPLE gathers outside, standing at
attention, forming their own tableau.

                    HOMELESS PEOPLE
          PEOPLE SCREAMING FOR THEIR TOAST

                    CAROLYN
          IN A SMALL, SOHO CAFE

The LINE COOKS step out of the kitchen en masse.

          LINE COOKS
    ON AN ISLAND IN

Everyone now joins together, creating a soaring, multi-part harmony, as Jon finishes arranging them into *La Grand Jette.*

          ALL

    TWO RIVERS

One last finishing touch, as Jon pulls a healthy Freddy out of the kitchen and adds him to the tableau.

          ALL (CONT'D)
    ON AN ORDINARY
    SUNDAY
    SUNDAY
    SUNDAY
    SUNDAY

          JON

    BRUNCH

INT. THEATER - NIGHT - 1992

Jon walks from the piano to the microphone at the lip of the stage. As he does, DRUMS come in underneath, a hip-hop BEAT.

          JON
    Monday morning. My first day of
    rehearsals for the *Superbia* workshop,
    which is still -- in case you'd
    forgotten -- missing its crucial Act
    Two musical number. I make my way
    there through the land of the dead:
    the Theater District.

EXT. TIMES SQUARE - DAY - 1990

Jon walks through a pre-Giuliani, pre-*Lion King* Times Square, past shuttered Broadway houses and seedy sex shops. Jon passes a beat-boxing BUSKER, with a pink baseball cap on the ground. Jon drops the change he has into the hat. As Jon continues on his way, the Busker launches into **PLAY GAME.**

          BUSKER
    WALK THROUGH TIMES SQUARE
    WHAT DO YOU SEE?
    UGLINESS WHERE ARCHITECTURE
    USED TO BE
    GLAMOUR AND STYLE
    ARE REPLACED BY GAUD
    LIKE THE SIXTY DOLLAR SPECTACLE
    IT'S A FRAUD
    THAT'S THE PLAY GAME
            (MORE)

                        BUSKER (CONT'D)
          WHY DO I WANT TO PLAY THE PLAY GAME
          THAT'S THE PLAY GAME
          MUST BE INSANE TO PLAY THE PLAY GAME

We FOLLOW the BUSKER through a sequence that plays like a hip-
hop music video circa 1990. The Busker, rapping, sounds exactly
the way that Jon imagines *he* sounds, rapping.

                        BUSKER (CONT'D)
          EVEN OFF BROADWAY
          THERE'S NO GUARANTEE
          THAT SOME MBA
          WON'T DECIDE WHAT YOU SEE
          JUST LIKE AMERICA
          LACKING INNOVATION
          JUST GETTING BY
          ON GLITZ AND REPUTATION
          JUST LIKE AMERICA
          ON THE DECLINE
          UNCONCERNED WITH PRODUCT
          JUST THE BOTTOM LINE
          YOU WANNA WRITE A PLAY?
          ARE YOU OUT OF YOUR MIND?
          THAT'S LIKE TRYING TO DRIVE A MACK
          TRUCK
          IF YOU'RE BLIND
          WRITE FOR THE MOVIES
          WRITE FOR T.V.
          SO WHAT IF IT'S CRAP
          AT LEAST YOU WON'T WRITE FOR FREE
          MAKE THOUSANDS OF DOLLARS
          FOR A FIRST DRAFT
          AND YOUR LIFE WON'T DEPEND
          ON WHETHER FRANK RICH LAUGHED
          SO JUST FORGET SHAKESPEARE
          BECKETT, MOLIERE
          THAT'S THE PLAY GAME --

INT. THEATER - NIGHT - 1992

Jon, wearing an identical pink hat turned to the side, raps
with a mic, hopelessly Caucasian.

                        JON
          THAT'S THE PLAY GAME
          WHY DO I WANT TO PLAY THE PLAY GAME
          THAT'S THE PLAY GAME
          MUST BE INSANE TO PLAY THE PLAY GAME

INT. REHEARSAL STUDIO HALLWAY - DAY - 1990

Jon moves down a hallway filled with ACTORS, SINGERS, and
DANCERS.

Without noticing him, Jon passes the Busker, who holds a headshot and resume and stands in a line of other Actors, waiting to check in with a CASTING DIRECTOR.

> BUSKER
> THAT'S THE PLAY GAME
> THAT'S THE PLAY GAME
> THAT'S THE PLAY GAME
> WHY DO I CARE?

Finally, the Busker reaches the front of the line, nods to the Casting Director. On the door, a sign: *Cats*, National Tour.

> BUSKER (CONT'D)
> I'll be reading for the role of Old Deuteronomy.

INT. REHEARSAL STUDIO - MINUTES LATER - 1990

In a small rehearsal room, Jon stands in a circle with the large CAST of *Superbia* -- including Roger, Karessa, Cristin, and Gerard -- as Ira Weitzman says a brief word.

> IRA
> On behalf of Playwrights Horizons, I just want to welcome everyone and thank you all for taking part in this very exciting new musical by a very exciting young writer, Jonathan Larson. He's not even *thirty*.

The Cast claps, amazed by this. Ira looks to Jon to say something. Jon steps forward, confident, at ease.

> JON
> Thank you, Ira. This is the first real workshop that this musical has ever had. So, now you guys are part of the family. Does anyone have any questions before we get going?

A beat. One actress, LAUREN (20s), finally raises his hand, timidly.

> LAUREN
> Can you, um... can you explain it, maybe?

> JON
> Explain what?

> LAUREN
> Just... the musical. The story.
> It's... a little bit confusing... in
> certain places.

Others nod at the suggestion. Lauren clarifies.

> LAUREN (CONT'D)
> Not in a bad way.

INT. THEATER - NIGHT - 1992

Jon stands at the microphone.

> JON
> *Superbia*. A satire set in the future
> on a poisoned planet Earth, where the
> vast majority of humanity spends their
> lives staring at the screens of their
> media transmitters, watching the tiny
> elite of the rich and powerful who
> film their own fabulous lives like TV
> shows. A world where human emotion has
> been outlawed. This will be the first
> musical for the MTV generation, this
> will be --

INT. REHEARSAL STUDIO - DAY - 1990

Back to Jon and the circle of actors.

> GERARD
> Is it supposed to be about aliens? I
> didn't know if it was supposed to be
> aliens...

> JON
> No, not aliens. But...it is set in the
> future. It's set in the future.

INT. REHEARSAL STUDIO - LATER - 1990

Cristin and Roger stand around the piano. Jon, at the piano,
plays **SEXTET.** He cues Cristin to begin singing.

> CRISTIN
> THE COLOR-SCHEME FOR THE DAY
> IS BLACK-RED-BLACK
> THE DRUG, OF COURSE,
> WILL BE THE KILOWATT
> THE TREND TODAY IS TO SAY
> THE ADJECTIVE "FUN" A LOT

                    JON
          It's perfect. Keep going.

                    CRISTIN
          STUDD STAR, YOU HAVE RECEIVED
          TWO NOMINATIONS
          "FACE OF THE YEAR"
          AND "BEST HAIR"
          PREPARE A SPEECH FOR YOUR PHOTO
          OPPORTUNITY
          YOUR AGENT TIM PURSENT WILL BE THERE

As the song continues to UNDERSCORE --

INT. REHEARSAL STUDIO - NIGHT - 1990

Jon huddles with Ira at the end of the day.

                    IRA
          You told me you needed a drummer --

                    JON
          No, I told you, I needed a band.

                    IRA
          It's a hundred dollars for every extra
          musician...

                    JON
          And your annual operating budget is...
          half a million dollars?

                    IRA
          So far we're up to twelve RSVPs, Jon.
          You don't need a band with an audience
          of twelve people -- you'll outnumber
          them.
              (then)
          If you want more musicians, you're
          going to have to find the money for it
          somewhere else. I'm sorry.

                    JON
          Thank you for everything.

INT. HOSPITAL - NIGHT - 1990

Jon and Carolyn sit, wearing surgical masks, beside Freddy --
asleep in his hospital bed, hooked up to a battery of machines.
Jon writes in his notepad, "Why aren't we fighting?"

                    JON (V.O.)
          I went to three friends' funerals last
          year. The oldest one was twenty-seven.
              (MORE)

JON (V.O.) (CONT'D)
Pam. Gordon. Allie. Freddy's not
even... he turned twenty-five two
weeks ago. And nobody is doing enough.
I'm not doing enough. There's not
enough time. Or maybe I'm just wasting
my time...

INT. JON'S BEDROOM - NIGHT - 1990

Jon, wiped out, comes home to find Susan in bed. He crawls in
next to her. She pulls him close.

JON (V.O.)
And what about Susan's time? When am I
going to talk to Susan? What am I
going to say? I don't know what to
say. So Susan waits. And time keeps on
ticking.

INT. JON'S APARTMENT - NIGHT - 1990

Jon sits in front of his computer.

JON (V.O.)
Tick, tick, tick. I have three days
left until the workshop. Three days
left to write this song. And if this
song doesn't work, the show doesn't
work, and then it's all been a waste
of time -- who gives a *shit* about a
song?

INT. JON'S APARTMENT - DAY - 1990

Jon stands in Michael's bedroom, empty, appearing even smaller
without furniture. The apartment feels lonelier than ever.

JON (V.O.)
I miss Michael. I want to talk to
Michael. I don't have time to talk to
Michael.

INT. REHEARSAL STUDIO - DAY - 1990

Jon, sitting behind the rehearsal Pianist, watches the Cast
perform "Sextet."

JON
(whispers, to Pianist)
Make sure you're not speeding up.

The door opens and Jon turns to see Susan enter. He turns back
to Pianist.

                         JON (CONT'D)
          I'm missing the consonants here.

Susan approaches him, whispering.

                         SUSAN
          It sounds great.

                         JON
          Why didn't you tell me you were
          coming?

                         SUSAN
          I guess, I thought it might be a nice
          surprise...

                         JON
          No, yeah, it is.

                         SUSAN
          It's Tuesday.
               (off his blank look)
          I have to give them my decision on the
          job by tomorrow. Do you have a break
          coming up so we can talk?

                         JON
          The actors have a break. I don't have
          any breaks.

                         SUSAN
          Well, I don't know what I'm going to
          do.

                         JON
          Can you ask for an extension? I'm
          sorry, I just -- can we talk about it
          tonight?
               (back to the Pianist)
          Let's add this whole section to the
          work list. Add the whole song.

Jon turns back to finish the conversation, but Susan is already
gone.

INT. REHEARSAL STUDIO - DAY - 1990

Jon watches Cristin and Roger perform, scripts in hand.

                         CRISTIN
          A NOMINATION

                         ROGER
          A NOMINATION?

                    CRISTIN
        NOMINATION FOR A FACE AWARD

                    ROGER
        A FACE AWARD?

                    CRISTIN
        LET'S PLUG IN

                    ROGER
        DOES THIS MEAN THAT I'LL BE ON THE
        AIR?

                    CRISTIN
        YOU ALREADY WERE
        LAST NIGHT, WHAT A SIGHT YOU WERE

                    ROGER
        I WAS?

                    CRISTIN
        YOU WERE
        YOU PLAYED WITH MY LASER
        YOU THOUGHT IT WAS A RAZOR
        I'M POSITIVE THAT'S WHAT CAUSED
        SUCH A SCENE

                    ROGER
        WE CAN GET ON THE AIR
        MY MUSIC BOX ON THE AIR
        WHERE? WHO? WHAT DOES THIS MEAN?

                    ROGER & CRISTIN
        EVERYONE WHO EVER HAS, OR
        EVER WILL BE ANYONE WILL BE THERE
        THE SOPHISTICATED, EFFERVESCENT,
        CHARISMATIC, INCANDESCENT, DEBONAIR
        THE EVENT OF THE CENTURY
        THE QUINTESSENTIAL SOCIAL ADVENTURE
        WE CANNOT AFFORD TO LET YOU MISS YOUR
        DEBUT
        THE 31ST ANNUAL FACE AWARD
        PRESENTATION CEREMONY
        LIVE, VIA SATELLITE, IN COLOR
        FROM THE MARVELOUS GLAMORAMA
        EVERYONE WILL BE THERE

The chilly staccato PIANO part continues to UNDERSCORE as --

INT. STRAND BOOK STORE - DUSK - 1990

Jon stands at the counter, as a buyer, MOLLY (50s) goes through
the milk crate of old books (Sontag, Neruda, Cage) and records
(Dylan, Sex Pistols, *Carmina Burana*) that Jon has dumped there.

                         MOLLY
          I can give you fifty for everything.

                         JON
          You're going to sell it for five times
          that.

                         MOLLY
          Fifty's the best I can do.

                         JON
               (a beat, then)
          Cash?

                         MOLLY
          Great.

She hands him the money. He stands there, staring at his
things, conflicted, then grabs the *Godspell* LP and goes.

                         MOLLY (CONT'D)
          Oh no. He's keeping the *Godspell*.

INT. JON'S APARTMENT / INT. MICHAEL'S APARTMENT - NIGHT - 1990

Jon, barely listening, talks on the phone to Michael as he
scribbles and erases rewrites in his script. Michael sits in
his half-furnished apartment, surrounded by moving boxes.

                         MICHAEL
          I'd love to take you to lunch,
          celebrate your birthday.

                         JON
          I can't this week.

                         MICHAEL
          I could really use your advice on some
          things...

Jon isn't listening at all.

                         JON
          Can I call you back later? I'm right
          in the middle of something here...

                         MICHAEL
          Oh, that focus group I mentioned.
          They're still looking for one more
          person to sign up. It's Thursday at
          eleven. I know money's tight for you
          right now...

Jon begins to pay attention.

                    MICHAEL (CONT'D)
          You know what? Never mind --

                    JON
          How much does it pay?

                    MICHAEL
          It's only seventy-five bucks, but...

                    JON
          I'll be there.

INT. YMCA POOL - NIGHT - 1990

Jon dives into the pool, the shock of cold water almost enough
to stop his racing thoughts.

INT. REHEARSAL STUDIO - NIGHT - 1990

Jon, his expression unreadable, watches the Cast perform
"Sextet" full-out, with a SYNTH PLAYER now added to the Pianist
and Drummer. Ira listens, in awe, blown away by how much better
it sounds with the Synth.

                    FULL CAST
          EVERYONE WHO EVER HAS, OR
          EVER WILL BE ANYONE WILL BE THERE

Ira whispers to Jon.

                    IRA
          You were right.

                    JON
          I know.

                    FULL CAST
          NEVER IN THE HISTORY OF ENTERTAINMENT
          WILL THERE BE AN AFFAIR - QUITE LIKE
          IT
          THE EVENT OF THE CENTURY
          THE QUINTESSENTIAL SOCIAL ADVENTURE
          WE CANNOT AFFORD TO MISS THIS NIGHT OF
          BLISS
          THE 31ST ANNUAL FACE AWARD
          PRESENTATION CEREMONY
          LIVE, VIA SATELLITE, IN COLOR
          IT'S AN 18 HOUR FUNCTION
          WITH COMMERCIAL INTERRUPTION
          FROM THE MARVELOUS, GLORIOUS, SLAM
          BANG GLAMORAMA
          EVERYONE WHO'S ANYONE KNOWS
          EVERYONE WHO'S ANYONE KNOWS
          EVERYONE WHO'S ANYONE KNOWS
                    (MORE)

FULL CAST   (CONT'D)
EVERYONE WHO'S ANYONE KNOWS
EVERYONE WHO'S ANYONE KNOWS
EVERYONE WILL BE THERE!

As they hit the final note, they look to Jon for his reaction.
He stands there for a moment, feeling the pressure, saying
nothing.

INT. REHEARSAL STUDIO - NIGHT - 1990

On a break, Jon sits with his head in his hands, as stressed as
he's ever been. Karessa passes.

                    KARESSA
          Can I hear it yet?
               (off his blank look)
          The new song...

                    JON
          Any day now.

                    KARESSA
          You're killing me, Larson...

As she goes, Jon's smile withers.

INT. JON'S APARTMENT - NIGHT - 1990

Jon sits at the keyboard, picking out various NOTES, searching
for the right melody. The phone RINGS. He ignores it, picks at
a sequence of NOTES on the keyboard -- G, B flat, A flat, G.
The machine picks up with Jon's outgoing MESSAGE.

                    JON (V.O.)
          Speak.

                    SUSAN
               (on the machine)
          Hey, it's me. Just pick up the phone.
               (then)
          I know you're screening your calls.
          Every light is on in your apartment
          right now.

Jon stands, peers out the window, sees Susan at the pay phone
across the street, looking up at him.

INT. JON'S APARTMENT - MINUTES LATER - 1990

Jon lets Susan into the apartment.

                    JON
          You could have called first.

                    SUSAN
          I just did. It's great to see you,
          too.

                    JON
          I didn't mean it like that.

Susan takes in the apartment for the first time: dirty dishes,
take-out boxes, old drafts of scripts, overflowing litter box.

                    SUSAN
          Jesus, Jonathan.

He says nothing.

                    SUSAN (CONT'D)
          I need you to talk to me.

                    JON
          I'm writing, Susan.

                    SUSAN
          You're going to write the great
          American musical in the next ten
          minutes?

                    JON
          Thank you for being so supportive of
          my work.

                    SUSAN
          Oh, because you're such a champion of
          mine.

                    JON
          What is that supposed to mean?

                    SUSAN
          What do you think it means?

As we PRE-LAP the sound of a drum ROLL...

INT. THEATER - NIGHT - 1992

Karessa and Jon pull their stools to the lip of the stage.

                    JON
          And now, ladies and gentlemen, we
          present you with: scenes from a modern
          romance. As told in song!

The CRASH of a cymbal, as the MUSIC for **THERAPY** creeps in, the
zippy, playful tone in stark contrast to Jon and Susan's
argument.

We INTERCUT throughout between the THEATER and the APARTMENT, the two in jagged juxtaposition.

- BACK TO APARTMENT

                    SUSAN
          I'm sorry -- I'm not allowed to talk
          about my needs. What needs?

                    JON
          Did I say that?

                    SUSAN
          You didn't have to say it. It's
          implied.

                    JON
          How is it implied?

                    SUSAN
          You're the artist. I'm the girlfriend.

- BACK TO THEATER

                    JON
          I FEEL BAD THAT YOU FEEL BAD
          ABOUT ME FEELING BAD, ABOUT YOU
          FEELING BAD
          ABOUT WHAT I SAID, ABOUT WHAT YOU SAID
          ABOUT ME NOT BEING ABLE TO SHARE A
          FEELING

- BACK TO APARTMENT

                    JON (CONT'D)
          Can we talk about this later? Please?

                    SUSAN
          When, Jonathan? When is later?

                    JON
          Not tonight.

- BACK TO THEATER

                    KARESSA
          IF I THOUGHT THAT WHAT YOU THOUGHT
          WAS THAT I HADN'T THOUGHT ABOUT
          SHARING MY THOUGHTS
          THEN MY REACTION TO YOUR REACTION
          TO MY REACTION
          WOULD HAVE BEEN MORE REVEALING

- BACK TO APARTMENT

                    JON
          I have been rehearsing all day. I have
          been up since four this morning. I
          have been trying to write a song for a
          week and I am *nowhere.*

- BACK TO THEATER

                    JON (CONT'D)
          I WAS AFRAID THAT YOU'D BE AFRAID
          IF I TOLD YOU THAT I WAS AFRAID OF
          INTIMACY

- BACK TO APARTMENT

                    SUSAN
          I've been telling you for months how
          unhappy I am.

- BACK TO THEATER

                    JON
          IF YOU DON'T HAVE A PROBLEM WITH MY
          PROBLEM
          MAYBE THE PROBLEM IS SIMPLY CO-
          DEPENDENCY

- BACK TO APARTMENT

                    JON (CONT'D)
          Everyone is unhappy in New York.
          That's what New York *is.*

- BACK TO THEATER

                    JON (CONT'D)
          I WAS WRONG TO

                    KARESSA
          SAY YOU WERE WRONG TO

                    JON
          SAY I WAS WRONG ABOUT

                    KARESSA
          YOU BEING WRONG

                    JON
          WHEN YOU RANG TO SAY THAT

                    KARESSA
          THE RING WAS THE WRONG THING TO BRING

                              JON
          IF I MEANT WHAT I SAID
          WHEN I SAID "RINGS BORE ME"

- BACK TO APARTMENT

                              SUSAN
          I don't know how to get through to you
          anymore. You keep shutting me out. You
          put up these fences --

                              JON
          I'm not shutting you out.

                              SUSAN
          You're a million miles away, all the
          time.

                              JON
          Actually, I'm right here.

                              SUSAN
          Are you, Jonathan? Actually?

- BACK TO THEATER

                        JON AND KARESSA
          I'M NOT MAD THAT YOU GOT MAD THAT I
          GOT MAD
          WHEN YOU SAID I SHOULD GO DROP DEAD

                              JON
          IF I WERE YOU AND I'D DONE WHAT I'D
          DONE
          I'D DO WHAT YOU DID WHEN I GAVE YOU
          THE RING
          HAVING SAID WHAT I SAID

- BACK TO APARTMENT

                         JON (CONT'D)
          You're right, I've been distracted,
          but I promise, after the workshop -- I
          just have to get to after the
          workshop...

                              SUSAN
          Everything is *after the workshop.*
               (then)
          What if the workshop happens and
          nothing changes? No producer with a
          big check. You don't go straight to
          Broadway.
                              (MORE)

> SUSAN (CONT'D)
> You're still a waiter, you're still
> living in this apartment, you're still
> broke. What then, Jonathan? And what
> about me?

- BACK TO THEATER

JON	KARESSA
I FEEL BAD, THAT YOU FEEL BAD	I FEEL BADLY ABOUT YOU
ABOUT ME FEELING BAD, ABOUT YOU	FEELING BADLY ABOUT ME
FEELING BAD	FEEL BADLY ABOUT YOU
ABOUT WHAT I SAID, ABOUT WHAT	
YOU SAID	
ABOUT ME NOT BEING ABLE TO	
SHARE A FEELING	

- BACK TO APARTMENT

> JON (CONT'D)
> I can't move to the Berkshires. I
> can't leave my career behind.

Susan looks at him, incredulous.

> SUSAN
> You think I don't know that?

> JON
> Then what are we even...? What do you
> want?

She laughs, sadly.

> SUSAN
> I guess I just wanted you to tell me
> not to go.

- BACK TO THEATER

JON	KARESSA
I THOUGHT YOU THOUGHT I REACTED	IF I THOUGHT THAT WHAT YOU
SHALLOWLY	THOUGHT
WHEN I REACTED TO YOU	WAS THAT I HADN'T THOUGHT ABOUT
	SHARING MY THOUGHTS
	THEN MY REACTION TO YOUR
	REACTION
	TO MY REACTION
	WOULD HAVE BEEN MORE REVEALING

- BACK TO APARTMENT

> JON (CONT'D)
> Of course I don't want you to go.

                         SUSAN
              Really?

                         JON
              Obviously.

                         SUSAN
              Because this is the first time you've
              said it.

Jon throws his arms around her. He holds her. And for a moment,
it seems as if all the anger and resentment and hurt have
simply vanished. And then, Susan realizes, with horror --

                         SUSAN (CONT'D)
              Oh my God.

- BACK TO THEATER

                         JON
              BUT NOW IT'S OUT IN THE OPEN

- BACK TO APARTMENT

                         SUSAN
              You're thinking about how to turn this
              into a song, aren't you?

- BACK TO THEATER

                         KARESSA
              NOW IT'S OFF OUR CHEST

- BACK TO APARTMENT

                         JON
                    (it's true)
              No. What?

                         SUSAN
              You know what, Jonathan? I'm done.

She goes to the door, Jon following lamely behind her.

                         JON
              Susan. Susan, wait.

                         SUSAN
              I hope you have an amazing workshop.

                         JON
              Susan. Hold on, Susan.

- BACK TO THEATER

> JON AND KARESSA
> NOW IT'S FOUR AM
> AND WE HAVE THERAPY TOMORROW

- BACK TO APARTMENT

Susan storms out, SLAMMING the door behind her.

- BACK TO THEATER

> JON AND KARESSA (CONT'D)
> IT'S TOO LATE TO SCREW

- BACK TO APARTMENT

Jon lets out his frustration by yelling at the wall.

> JON
> *Shit.*

- BACK TO THEATER

> JON AND KARESSA
> SO LET'S JUST GET SOME REST

The song BUTTONS and the Audience APPLAUDS wildly, a good time
had by all.

INT. OFFICE CONFERENCE ROOM - DAY - 1990

A table in a sleek corporate conference room. Already assembled
there, dressed in impeccable business attire and wearing name-
tags are: PEGGY (20s), TODD (40s), and KIM (50s). At the front
of the room, JUDY (30s), standing beside a large easel pad,
checks the time.

> JUDY
> We're just waiting on one more
> person...

Looking the worse for wear after a night without sleep and
dressed in a hastily assembled outfit of jeans and a t-shirt,
Jon appears at the door.

> JON
> Hi, I'm Jonathan --

> JUDY
> Yes. Mr. Larson. You're Michael's
> friend.

> JON
> How are you?

                         JUDY
               You're late.

                         JON
               Okay, sorry about that.

She holds open the door, gesturing for him to take a seat. Jon
nods to the others and sits. Kim smiles at him.

                         KIM
               Welcome.

As Judy stands in front of the table beside a large easel pad,
Jon leans over to Peggy, whispering.

                         JON
               Did she say anything about when we get
               paid?

She ignores him, doesn't want to be associated with the late
guy.

                         JUDY
               So. Now that we're all here... why
               don't we begin with a quick
               brainstorming session? Just to get
               those creative juices flowing.

                         JON (V.O.)
               Two hours of this.

INT. THEATER - NIGHT - 1992

Jon stands at the front of the stage at the mic.

                         JON
               For one extra musician.

INT. OFFICE CONFERENCE ROOM - DAY - 1990

                         JUDY
               So why don't we just start by throwing
               out some ideas that come to mind when
               I say the word "America"?

                         PEGGY
               George Washington.

                         JUDY
               Excellent.

Judy writes the ideas on the pad as they are called out.

                              TODD
                    Abraham Lincoln.

                              JON (V.O.)
                         (in his head)
                    Empire, racism, genocide, Vietnam...
                         (out loud)
                    Grover Cleveland.

A slight pause. Judy nods, writes this on the pad.

                              KIM
                    The Constitution?

                              JUDY
                    Yes.

                              JON
                    Magna Carta.

Another slight pause. Judy nods, writes down the suggestion.
Jon suddenly realizes that he's losing.

                              PEGGY
                    The Bill of Rights.

                              TODD
                    The right thing to do.

                              KIM
                    The right stuff.

                              JON
                    An open road at sunset. The wind in
                    your hair. Nothing in your way but the
                    horizon.

Judy turns to look at him. A beat. Unclear what she's thinking.
Finally --

                              JUDY
                    That is beautiful, Mr. Larson.

Jon can't help but swell with the compliment.

INT. CONFERENCE ROOM - MINUTES LATER - 1990

A series of QUICK SHOTS of people at the table, one by one, as
they give rapid-fire answers.

                              PEGGY
                    The sun.

                    TODD
Sunrise.

                    JON
The dawn of a new day.

                    JUDY
That is incredible.

                    PEGGY
A window looking out on a field.

                    KIM
Aww. I think of cute little bunnies
and cute little squirrelys.

                    JON
The beating heart of the nation.

                    JUDY
         (savoring this)
Mmm. Absolutely.

Jon watches as Judy picks up her clipboard, circles his name.

                    JON (V.O.)
I could get used to this.

INT. THEATER - NIGHT - 1992

Jon begins to daydream at the microphone.

                    JON
I could get *paid* for this. I could get
health care, a 401K, a BMW, a luxury
apartment on Central Park West -- no,
no, no -- *East*. I could actually be
rewarded for my creativity, instead of
rejected and ignored.

INT. CONFERENCE ROOM - MINUTES LATER - 1990

Jon smiles to himself, as Judy tears off the current sheet on
the easel pad, a new, blank sheet underneath.

                    JON (V.O.)
This could be the rest of my life.

                    JUDY
Now that we have all of those fabulous
ideas of yours in our heads, we are
going to turn to our real task.
                    (MORE)

                         JUDY (CONT'D)
          We are here to develop the name for a
          revolutionary consumer product that is
          just about to hit your shelves.

                         KIM
          Oh wow.

                         JUDY
          This is where we're going to need that
          incredible imagination of yours, Mr.
          Larson.
               (then)
          The product we are looking at is a
          tasteless, odorless chemical compound
          that will be used as a fat substitute
          in cooking. It's been tested
          successfully on a number of mammals...

Jon begins to get a queasy feeling about this.

                         JUDY (CONT'D)
          Now there are some side effects
          associated with the product that I've
          been instructed to tell you about...

Jon realizes with a shudder:

                         JON (V.O.)
          This could be the rest of my life.

Judy finishes reading the long list of side effects.

                         JUDY
          ... and finally, in a small number of
          users, there were reports of toxic
          shock syndrome, resulting in brief
          hospitalization.

She plasters the wide smile back on.

                         JUDY (CONT'D)
          There are no bad ideas.

Jon suddenly notices the large wall clock above her for the
first time -- TICK, TICK, TICK. His breathing gets shallower.

                         PEGGY
          Free Oil.

                         JUDY
          Love it.

                         KIM
          Oil Free.

                         JON
          That's the same thing she just said.

                         KIM
                    (defensive)
          I switched the words around, though.

                         JUDY
                    (a look to Jon)
          That's perfectly fine, Kim, thank you.

Jon stares at the clock, as the ideas come furiously from
everyone else. He seems to be able to feel brain cells dying.

                         PEGGY
          The American Dream.

                         KIM
          Dreams of Freedom.

                         TODD
          Nutra Oil.

                         JUDY
          That's not bad, Todd.

Finally, Jon interjects, loudly, enthusiastically.

                         JON
          I've got it. I have it. I know exactly
          what it should be.

Everyone looks to him expectantly. He emphasizes each syllable.

                         JON (CONT'D)
          "Chubstitute."

EXT. MIDTOWN STREET - NIGHT - 1990

Michael and Jon walk down a busy sidewalk toward the subway,
the street teeming with rush hour traffic, Michael furious.

                         MICHAEL
          "Chubstitute."

                         JON
          It was a joke.

                         MICHAEL
          It's not funny.

                         JON
          Maybe not to you...

                    MICHAEL
          I recommended you, Jon. I put my name
          on the line for you.

                    JON
          Tell them I had a stroke.

                    MICHAEL
               (exploding)
          It isn't *funny*.

Jon goes silent, surprised by his response, as Michael stops
there on the sidewalk, turns to him.

                    MICHAEL (CONT'D)
          This is my life.

                    JON
          It's not your life. It's advertising.
          It's figuring out how to trick people
          into buying shit they don't want.

                    MICHAEL
          Actually, it's a lot more complicated
          than that.

                    JON
          I don't understand how you can take
          any of this seriously.

                    MICHAEL
          Because they pay me to.

                    JON
          Money isn't everything.

                    MICHAEL
          Well, it doesn't hurt.

                    JON
          Are you sure about that?

                    MICHAEL
          What are you doing with your life
          that's so noble?

                    JON
          Making art.

                    MICHAEL
          Oh, that's what the world needs. More
          art.

                    JON
          Actually yes, and at least I'm not
          helping perpetuate a system that is
          destroying --

                    MICHAEL
          Oh spare me the self-righteousness,
          Jon. You're writing musicals in your
          living room, not saving the rain
          forest.

                    JON
          Wow. I wish I could be more like you
          and spend my life caring about driving
          the right car and wearing the right
          suits and living in a doorman
          building...

                    MICHAEL
          Why shouldn't I care about those
          things? Not everyone has the *options*
          you do, Jon. All the things you take
          for granted.

                    JON
          Like what?

                    MICHAEL
          Like, a life with a person you love.
          Do you know what I would give to have
          that? And you turn your nose up at it.

                    JON
          If that's what you want, what's
          stopping you?

                    MICHAEL
          What's stopping me? How about Jesse
          Helms and the Moral Majority? How
          about the people that run this
          country? I can't get married. I can't
          have kids. Half of our friends are
          dying, and the other half are scared
          to death they're next. So, yes, I'm
          sorry for buying a nice car, Jon. I'm
          sorry for living in an apartment with
          central heating. I'm sorry for
          enjoying my life while I still have
          time.
               (stops himself)
          I have to go.

He heads off in the opposite direction.

                          JON
              You're not taking the subway?

                          MICHAEL
              I'd rather walk.

                          JON
              Michael. Michael.

But Michael just keeps going. As Jon watches him disappear down
the sidewalk, there it is again -- TICK, TICK, TICK.

INT. JON'S APARTMENT - NIGHT - 1990

Jon arrives home at the apartment to find the phone RINGING. He
picks it up.

                          JON
              Hello?

INT. ROSA STEVENS' OFFICE - NIGHT - 1990

ROSA STEVENS (50s, old school, salty) sits at her cluttered
desk, smoking a cigarette, as she talks on the phone to him.

                          ROSA (ON PHONE)
              Jonny, darling, it's Rosa.

INTERCUT throughout between Jon and Rosa.

                          JON (ON PHONE)
                  (stunned)
              Rosa Stevens?

                          ROSA (ON PHONE)
              Are we excited for tomorrow?

                          JON (ON PHONE)
              Tomorrow? The presentation? You
              remembered the presentation?

                          ROSA (ON PHONE)
              Remembered it? I've got every producer
              in town coming. So it better be good.

Wonderful. More pressure.

                          JON (ON PHONE)
              Yes, it's... it's going to be great.

                          ROSA (ON PHONE)
              Let's see if we can't get a bidding
              war started on this musical of yours,
              what do you say?

>   JON (ON PHONE)
>   That's... that would be... yes.
>
>   ROSA (ON PHONE)
>   Okay, doll.
>   (shouts, to Assistant)
>   Let's get Hal Prince on the phone.
>
>   JON (ON PHONE)
>   Rosa?

She's gone. Jon hangs up the phone, takes a deep breath, feeling a new determination.

INT. JON'S APARTMENT - NIGHT - 1990

A SERIES OF SHOTS as Jon prepares to get to work.

- Jon takes a garbage bag, goes through the apartment, picking up the debris.

- Jon empties Finster's litter box, shirt pulled over his nose to block the smell.

>   JON
>   (to Finster)
>   I'm so sorry.

- Jon vacuums.

- Jon pours fresh grounds into the coffee machine.

- Jon stands in the bathroom, considering the Victoria's Secret catalogue, when Finster pokes his head in the door. Jon guiltily sets down the catalogue, begins to exit.

>   JON (CONT'D)
>   Okay, I'm going, I'm going...

- Jon presses the switch and his Macintosh computer HUMS to life.

- Jon flicks on his keyboard.

- Jon pours himself a cup of steaming hot coffee.

INT. JON'S APARTMENT - LATER - 1990

In the freshly cleaned living room, Jon sits at the keyboard. He takes a breath, focusing. His hands hover over the keys, ready to get to work, when all at once the LIGHTS cut out.

INT. JON'S APARTMENT - MINUTES LATER - 1990

Standing in the dark, on the phone, Jon -- in a state --
pleads. A MAN'S VOICE comes through the receiver.

                    JON (ON PHONE)
          Why wouldn't you have called to tell
          me that my payment was late *before* you
          cut off my power? How does that make
          sense?

                    MAN'S VOICE
          Sir, as I explained before, you
          received a notice in the mail --

                    JON (ON PHONE)
          You don't understand. I have a
          workshop -- a public presentation of
          my musical in twelve hours.

                    MAN'S VOICE
          Sir --

                    JON (ON PHONE)
          I can pay you over the phone right
          now. I have my credit card right here.

                    MAN'S VOICE
          The billing office is closed for the
          night.

                    JON (ON PHONE)
              (loses it)
          What am I supposed to do?

                    MAN'S VOICE
              (a beat)
          Sir, like I said, call --

He hangs up. A beat. He dials another number. The phone RINGS
twice, before Susan's roommate BETH answers. We hear her VOICE
through the receiver.

                    BETH'S VOICE
          Hello?

                    JON (ON PHONE)
              (turning on the charm)
          Hey, Beth. How are you? It's Jon.

                    BETH'S VOICE
              (cold)
          Hi, Jon.

>   JON (ON PHONE)
>   Is Susan there?

>   BETH'S VOICE
>   She doesn't want to talk to you, Jon.

He can't exactly blame her.

>   JON (ON PHONE)
>   Can you give her a message for me?

>   BETH'S VOICE
>   What is it?

>   JON (ON PHONE)
>   I wanted to remind her that tomorrow's
>   my workshop and I know I don't have
>   any right to ask this, but I just... I
>   would really love her to be there.

>   BETH'S VOICE
>   (a beat)
>   I'll tell her you called.

INT. THEATER - NIGHT - 1992

As the driving DRUM and jittery BASS intro of **SWIMMING** begins,
Jon sits at the piano, on the microphone.

>   JON
>   Here I am. The musical to which I have
>   given my youth is about to be put on
>   public display for every producer in
>   New York. I haven't written a single
>   note or a single lyric of the most
>   important song in the show. I have no
>   electricity. My best friend is furious
>   with me. My girlfriend isn't speaking
>   to me. And there's only one thing I
>   can think of to do: swim.

INT. YMCA LOCKER ROOM - NIGHT - 1990

Jon listens to a Walkman, as he changes in the dank, filthy
locker room, surrounded by a half dozen other MEN in various
states of undress, lost entirely in his own thoughts.

>   JON (V.O.)
>   I HATE THIS LOCKER ROOM
>   WHY WON'T SUSAN ANSWER MY CALLS?
>   SWEAT WET ECHOES
>   SMELL HELL RAP

He pulls off his shirt. A locker slams shut. He turns up the
volume on the Walkman.

                         JON (V.O.)
                    PUMP UP THE VOLUME
                    HOT, WET, HOT, SWEAT

INT. YMCA POOL - MINUTES LATER - 1990

Jon stands by the edge of the pool, putting on his swim cap --
a few SWIMMERS doing laps.

                         JON (V.O.)
                    HOW'S THE WATER? STRETCH STRETCH
                    SPIT IN THE MASK

He spits in his goggles.

                         JON (V.O.)
                    CLOUDY VISION

He puts them on, dips his foot in the water.

                         JON (V.O.)
                    TEST THE WATER
                    CONTEMPLATE THE DIVE
                    THE SHOCK TO THE SKIN
                    ANTICIPATE THE PAIN THE PAIN THE PAIN
                    THE PAIN THE PAIN NOW

He DIVES in...

INT. YMCA POOL - MINUTES LATER - 1990

He swims laps at an aggressively fast pace.

                         JON (V.O.)
                    1, 2, 3 OH BITE THE AIR -- SEVEN

As he comes in and out of the water, vision blurry, he sees a
WOMAN (30s) standing by the side of the pool.

                         JON (V.O.)
                    THERE'S THAT GIRL -- 1, 2, 3, OH BITE
                    THE AIR
                    SMOOTH SOFT SKIN -- 2, 3, OH BITE THE -
                    - 13
                    LONG LEGS, BROWN SKIN, AND WET HAIR
                    WHOA OH AND WET HAIR
                    HAS ROSA EVEN LISTENED TO MY TAPE?
                    KICK, STRETCH, WINDMILL ARMS
                    SEE THE HAND, POINT THE FEET
                    PULL -- WET HAIR -- RELAX,
                    THIS GUY'S TOO SLOW -- FIFTEEN
                              (MORE)

                              JON (V.O.)   (CONT'D)
                    CAN I MAKE IT TO FORTY
                    TOO SLOW

He's swimming as fast as he can now, driving his body to the
brink of exhaustion. His vision becomes blurrier, and as he
emerges from the water every few seconds to breathe, <u>the Woman</u>
<u>beside the pool seems to transform into Susan, then back to the</u>
<u>Woman, then back to Susan, and so on, a trick of the light.</u>

                              JON (V.O.)
                    TOUCH HIS HEEL -- MOVE
                    ANSWER MY CALLS!
                    RED GREEN STRIPES -- 50 FEET -- 60
                    FEET
                    SHE LOOKS LIKE SUSAN
                    DOES SHE KNOW I'M --
                    LOOK AT THE CURVE OF --
                    SUSAN'S BEAUTIFUL

Jon's pace becomes punishing.

                              JON (V.O.)
                    1, 2, 3, OH BITE THE AIR - SEVENTEEN
                    THERE SHE IS - 1, 2, 3, OH BITE THE
                    AIR
                    SMOOTH SOFT SKIN - 2, 3, OH BITE THE --
                    TWENTY NINE
                    LONG LEGS, BROWN SKIN AND
                    WET HAIR
                    WHOA OH
                    AND WET HAIR
                    OUT, DON'T THINK - OUT, OUT, LET IT
                    OUT
                    KEEP THE SHOULDER DOWN, DOWN
                    EASY - NOT TOO HARD
                    FIND THE MOVEMENT'S ORIGIN
                    FINGERS - NO, HANDS - NO
                    SHOULDER - NO, ELBOW - NO, NO
                    THIRTY-SIX - FROM THE BACK, YES
                    LOWER - THIRTY-NINE - FORTY
                    CENTER, CENTER

As he hits forty laps, he stops, drained, empty. He lets go,
allowing his body to sink. As he reaches the bottom, he begins
to notice the lines on the tiles start to shift, blurring,
unraveling, slowly rearranging themselves into a musical staff.
Notes begin to spill across the staff. His song.

                              JON (V.O.)
                    AHHHHHH

                              JON (V.O.)
                    FORWARD MOTION
                    THROUGH THE WATER

                         KARESSA (V.O.)
          COME TO YOUR SENSES

                         JON (V.O.)
               ESCAPE

                         ROGER (V.O.)
          COME TO YOUR SENSES

                         KARESSA (V.O.)
          COME TO YOUR SENSES

                         JON (V.O.)
          I AM SOARING
          I'M THE WATER

                         KARESSA (V.O.)
          YOU AS THE KNIGHT

                         ROGER (V.O.)
          YOU'RE ON THE AIR

                         JON (V.O.)
               ESCAPE

                         ROGER (V.O.)
          I'M UNDERGROUND

                         KARESSA (V.O.)
          ME AS THE QUEEN

Jon comes to the surface, pulls himself out of the water, and
walks quickly to the locker room. As the MUSIC continues --

INT. JON'S APARTMENT - NIGHT - 1990

Jon sits in the dark, a flashlight on his desk the only
illumination, scribbling on music manuscript paper.

INT. REHEARSAL STUDIO - DAY - 1990

The rehearsal room has been set up for a reading -- folding
chairs and music stands. Jon stands in the empty room,
anxiously waiting, sheet music for his brand new song in hand.

                         JON (V.O.)
               The show is about to begin. The room
               is completely empty. The show is about
               to begin and I am looking at sixty
               empty folding chairs.

Karessa walks in.

                    KARESSA
          Hey, boy genius.

                    JON
          I'm turning thirty on Sunday, you
          know?

                    KARESSA
          Oh. Well, Happy Birthday.

                    JON
               (unenthused)
          Thank you.

                    KARESSA
          Thirty is still young.

                    JON
          No one's here.

                    KARESSA
          It's not even nine. The presentation
          doesn't start until ten.

Jon laughs, realizing, relieved.

                    JON
          Can you sight-read?

He hands her the sheet music.

                    JON (V.O.)
          Slowly, miraculously, people start to
          show up.

INT. REHEARSAL STUDIO - LATER - 1990

Jon hugs his mother, NAN, as his father, AL, holds her coat. A
dozen or so Audience Members have already taken seats.

                    AL
          This is just phenomenal. Look at this
          space. It's phenomenal.

                    JON
          It's a rehearsal studio, Dad.

                    AL
          It's a *Broadway* rehearsal studio. This
          is the real thing.

                    NAN
          We're very excited for you, dear.

                    AL
          (lowers his voice)
     Are they paying you?

                    JON
     No.

                    NAN
     Next time.

Al spots a seat in the second row, a hand-made RESERVED sign on
it. He goes to sit in it.

                    JON
     That's for someone else actually.

                    NAN
          (a look to Al)
     Do you like that?

Jon gestures to the empty room.

                    JON
     You can literally sit in *any other
     seat.*

INT. REHEARSAL STUDIO - LATER - 1990

Half the seats are now taken, and the room is alive with
CHATTER and anticipation, as Michael approaches Jon, some
trepidation between them after the way they last left things.

                    MICHAEL
     Good turnout.

                    JON
     Yeah. It's mostly friends.

                    MICHAEL
          (sarcastic)
     What a nightmare.

                    JON
          (smiles, a beat)
     Thank you. For coming.

                    MICHAEL
     Wild horses, Jon. You know that...

As Michael takes a seat, Jon glances at the Reserved seat,
still empty. He checks his watch.

INT. REHEARSAL STUDIO - LATER - 1990

The room is now nearly full. Rosa Stevens enters. She looks around. Jon watches her approach a random man.

                    ROSA
          Jonathan. How are you?

As the man turns around, confused, Jon races to save him.

                    JON
          Rosa. Jon Larson...

                    ROSA
              (plays it off)
          There he is. Just the man I'm looking
          for. Are you nervous? Don't be
          nervous.

                    JON
          I'm a little nervous.

                    ROSA
          Of course you're nervous. The first
          presentation of your musical is like
          having a colonoscopy in the middle of
          Times Square. Only, with a
          colonoscopy, the worst thing that
          could happen is, you find out you have
          cancer. With a musical, you find out
          you're already dead.

INT. REHEARSAL STUDIO - LATER - 1990

The room is now packed. Jon stands on the side of the room, glancing anxiously from the door to the still-empty seat with the Reserved sign. Ira approaches him.

                    IRA
          We can't keep waiting. It's quarter
          past.

Jon finally nods. Ira puts a hand on his shoulder.

                    IRA (CONT'D)
          Break a leg.

Ira takes the Reserved sign off the seat and sits. Jon finally accepts that Susan isn't coming. He looks around the packed room, steeling himself to say something.

                    JON
          Hi. Good morning. Thank you. Welcome.
          I'm Jonathan Larson.

Michael leads the applause. The rest of the room slowly joins.

> JON (CONT'D)
> That's, you really don't have to do
> that... That's very kind. Thank you.
> Okay. Thank you all so much for being
> here this morning --

The door OPENS and Jon turns, expecting to see Susan there.
Instead, in walks Stephen Sondheim. He ducks into a seat in the
back row. Jon takes a moment to recover from his shock.

> JON (CONT'D)
> Right. Like I was saying, thank you.
> This is my musical, *Superbia*. I've
> been working on it for... a little
> while now. I really hope you like it.

APPLAUSE as Jon finds a seat in the front row.

INT. THEATER - NIGHT - 1992

Jon sits at the piano.

> JON
> And the next hour and a half are a
> blur.

INT. REHEARSAL STUDIO - DAY - 1990

CLOSE ON Jon, watching the show. All we see is his face, stoic,
unreadable.

> JON (V.O.)
> Then Karessa steps forward to sing the
> new song, not even twelve hours old.

INT. THEATER - NIGHT - 1992

Jon sits at the piano, as Karessa approaches the microphone at
the lip of the stage.

> JON
> I close my eyes. I brace myself. I
> don't dare take a breath.

INT. REHEARSAL STUDIO - DAY - 1990

From behind, we see the figure of Karessa set her music stand
at a microphone downstage, mirroring her movements from the
concert in 1992.

                         JON (V.O.)
               But when I open my eyes, I don't see
               Karessa there.

Jon opens his eyes. REVERSE to find --

EXT. ROOF - NIGHT - 1990

Susan stands on the roof. Jon sits in a folding chair, watching
as she sings **COME TO YOUR SENSES**.

                         SUSAN
               YOU'RE ON THE AIR,
               I'M UNDERGROUND
               SIGNAL'S FADING,
               CAN'T BE FOUND
               I FINALLY OPEN UP
               FOR YOU I WOULD DO ANYTHING
               BUT YOU'VE TURNED OFF THE VOLUME
               JUST WHEN I'VE BEGUN TO SING
               COME TO YOUR SENSES
               DEFENSES ARE NOT THE WAY TO GO
               AND YOU KNOW,
               OR AT LEAST YOU KNEW
               CAN'T YOU RECALL
               WHEN THIS ALL BEGAN
               IT WAS ONLY YOU AND ME
               IT WAS ONLY ME AND YOU

INT. REHEARSAL STUDIO - DAY - 1990

Karessa sings in the reading.

                         KARESSA
               I HAVE TO LAUGH
               WE SURE PUT ON A SHOW
               LOVE IS PASSÉ IN THIS DAY AND AGE
               HOW CAN WE EXPECT IT TO GROW?
               YOU AS THE KNIGHT
               ME AS THE QUEEN
               ALL I'VE GOT TONIGHT
               IS STATIC ON A SCREEN

EXT. ROOF - NIGHT - 1990

Susan sings.

                         SUSAN
               COME TO YOUR SENSES
               SUSPENSE IS FINE
               IF YOU'RE JUST AN EMPTY IMAGE
               EMANATING OUT OF A SCREEN
               BABY BE REAL,
               YOU CAN FEEL AGAIN
                         (MORE)

                    SUSAN (CONT'D)
          YOU DON'T NEED A MUSIC BOX MELODY
          TO KNOW WHAT I MEAN

INT. REHEARSAL STUDIO - DAY - 1990

Karessa sings.

                    KARESSA
          DEEP IN MY EYES,
          WHAT DO YOU SEE
          DEEP IN MY SIGHS,
          LISTEN TO ME

Susan and Karessa sing in harmony, as we begin to INTERCUT
between the Studio and the Roof.

                    KARESSA AND SUSAN
          LET THE MUSIC COMMENCE FROM INSIDE
          NOT ONLY ONE SENSE, BUT USE ALL FIVE
          COME TO YOUR SENSES
          COME TO YOUR SENSES
          COME TO YOUR SENSES
          BABY COME BACK ALIVE

INT. REHEARSAL STUDIO - DAY - 1990

An explosion of APPLAUSE rings out and Jon looks to the front
of the room, where Karessa now bows. Jon smiles at the raucous
response to the song, but he cannot help but feel a pang of
something else -- something like regret.

INT. JON'S APARTMENT - LATER - 1990

Jon paces, staring at the phone, waiting for it to RING.
Finally, it does. He answers immediately.

                    JON (ON PHONE)
          Hello?

INT. ROSA STEVENS' OFFICE - CONTINUOUS - 1990

Rosa sits at her desk, on the call.

                    ROSA (ON PHONE)
          Hi, honey, it's Rosa.

INTERCUT throughout between them. Jon sighs in relief.

                    JON (ON PHONE)
          Thank you so much for calling.

                    ROSA (ON PHONE)
          Well, you've already left six
          messages.

> JON (ON PHONE)
> Have you heard anything yet?

> ROSA (ON PHONE)
> Honey, I have heard *nothing but raves*.
> I'm getting call after call after
> call.

> JON (ON PHONE)
> Wow. Okay. That's great news.

> ROSA (ON PHONE)
> Everybody is telling me the same
> thing: "That Jonathan Larson -- I
> can't wait to see what he does next."

> JON (ON PHONE)
> What do you mean what I do next? What
> about *Superbia*?

Rosa acts like they have discussed this already, like she
didn't predict a bidding war fifteen hours ago.

> ROSA (ON PHONE)
> I always told you this was a tough
> sell. It's too arty for Broadway --
> tourists aren't going to shell out
> fifty dollars to see a show about
> spaceships and robots...

> JON (ON PHONE)
> Well, that's not what it's about.

> ROSA (ON PHONE)
> Well, of course *I* know that, Jonathan.
> But these producers, they care about
> one thing and one thing only...

> JON (ON PHONE)
> What about Off-Broadway?

> ROSA (ON PHONE)
> It's too expensive for Off. You've got
> a cast of thousands, special
> effects...

She puts her hand over the phone, calls to her Assistant.

> ROSA (ON PHONE) (CONT'D)
> Tell him I'll be on in a second.
>   (to Jon)
> Listen, sweetie, I've got to run.
> Congratulations on a terrific
> presentation.

                    JON (ON PHONE)
          But what am I supposed to do now?

Rosa frowns, confused by the question -- isn't it obvious?

                    ROSA (ON PHONE)
          You start writing the next one. And
          after you finish that one, you start
          the next. And on and on. That's what
          it is to be a writer, honey. You just
          keep throwing them against the wall
          and hoping against hope that
          eventually something sticks.
                    (then)
          Listen. A little advice from someone
          that's been in this business a long,
          long time? On the next one... maybe
          try writing about what you know.

Jon looks around at his tiny, dingy apartment, the world he
knows.

INT. MICHAEL'S OFFICE - DAY - 1990

Michael stands by his desk in a small-ish office, on the phone.

                    MICHAEL (ON PHONE)
          I think let's give it a minute and see
          what happens next week...

Jon enters.

                    JON
          I need a job. I'll apologize to the
          focus group lady. I'll never say
          anything bad about marketing research
          ever again, I swear to God.

                    MICHAEL (ON PHONE)
          I'm going to call you right back.

He hangs up the phone.

                    JON
          I want to do what you do. I want to
          have what you have. I want the BMW, I
          want the doorman, I want all of it.

                    MICHAEL
          What is going on?

                         JON
          I spent eight years killing myself on
          a musical that is never going to
          happen.

                         MICHAEL
          I find that very hard to believe. It
          was incredible this morning...

                         JON
          Well, not incredible enough.
                (then)
          I can't do it again, Mike. I can't
          stomach five more years of waiting
          tables, five more years of writing
          things that no one will ever see while
          Broadway just churns out mega-musicals
          without a hint of anything original or
          interesting or, God forbid, something
          to actually *say* about the *world*.

Michael allows him to go on, patiently. When he's finished, he
calmly responds.

                         MICHAEL
          Are you done?

                         JON
          No, actually --

                         MICHAEL
                (cutting him off)
          The presentation was... Jon, it was
          amazing. It would be a tragedy to give
          up what you have.

                         JON
          You did it.

                         MICHAEL
          Please. I was a mediocre actor -- do
          you know how many mediocre actors
          there are in New York City? Do you
          know how many Jonathan Larsons there
          are? One.

                         JON
          I can't keep wasting my time, Mike. I
          turn thirty in two days.

                         MICHAEL
          And?

                    JON
          Stephen Sondheim was twenty-seven when
          he had his first musical on Broadway.

                    MICHAEL
          Well, guess what? You're not Stephen
          Sondheim. You're going to have to wait
          a little bit longer...

Jon begins to spiral.

                    JON
          I can't keep waiting. This is my life.

                    MICHAEL
          I understand.

                    JON
          You don't understand. I'm running out
          of time.

                    MICHAEL
              (scoffs)
          You are not running out of time.

                    JON
          You don't know anything about it.

                    MICHAEL
              (quietly)
          I'm HIV positive.

A long, terrible silence.

                    JON
          What?
              (Michael says nothing)
          How long have you...?

                    MICHAEL
          A few days.
              (then)
          Who knows? I might get lucky. People
          do. They live a year, longer even.
              (a stoic smile)
          Anyway. I think I might know a thing
          or two about running out of time.

Jon stands there, reeling, as the TICKING returns.

                    JON
          Why didn't you tell me sooner?

Michael gives him a look. Jon realizes, with a sickened feeling.

> JON (CONT'D)
> You tried.

Michael's phone BUZZES. The voice of his ASSISTANT.

> MICHAEL'S ASSISTANT
> Jill Kramer, returning, on line 2.

Michael clears his throat.

> MICHAEL
> I have to take that.

> JONATHAN
> Michael --

> MICHAEL
> I can't talk about this now. Please.

Jon nods, weakly. Michael gathers himself, picks up the phone, as Jon turns and goes out the door...

INT. ELEVATOR - MINUTES LATER - 1990

Jon stands in a CROWDED elevator, surrounded by laughing, chit-chatting EMPLOYEES. The TICKING grows louder and louder.

INT. THEATER - NIGHT - 1992

Jon sits at the piano, silent, shocked. Finally --

> JON
> I think of the day I met Michael.

INT. ELEVATOR - MINUTES LATER - 1990

Jon stands there, listening to the TICKING.

> JON (V.O.)
> It was the first day at sleep-away
> camp twenty-two years ago. We were
> eight. I think of high school. All the
> shows we did together.

Jon begins to hear something else --

INT. MICHAEL'S OFFICE - DAY - FLASHBACK - 1990

Days earlier, Michael stands, staring out the window, reeling. He holds the phone away from his ear, struggling to process the news he has just heard. He sings **REAL LIFE.**

                              MICHAEL
                    IS THIS REAL LIFE?

INT. THEATER - NIGHT - 1992

Jon at the mic.

                              JON
                    I think of the summer our families
                    decided to stay in the same town in
                    Cape Cod, a mile away from each other.
                    We'd meet at the beach every night.
                    We'd sit there, talking until three in
                    the morning. About our plans.
                    How some day we would move to the city
                    together, find a cheap apartment, and
                    be discovered, and change the world...

EXT. MIDTOWN PHONE BOOTH - MINUTES LATER - 1990

Jon stands in a phone booth, receiver to his ear, listening as
an answering machine picks up on the other end.

                         SUSAN'S VOICE
                       (from phone)
                    Hey, you've reached Susan, Beth,
                    Gordon, and Monique.

EXT. MIDTOWN STREET - CONTINUOUS - 1990

Jon trudges down 5th Avenue, the sky growing darker, day
turning to night.

                              JON (V.O.)
                    I think of the first summer back from
                    college. We smoked a bowl on the
                    Kennedy breakwater and Michael told me
                    he was gay.

                              MICHAEL (V.O.)
                    IS THIS REAL LIFE?
                    IS THIS REAL LIFE?
                    IS THIS REAL LIFE?

EXT. CENTRAL PARK - MINUTES LATER - 1990

Jon is in the Park now, walking faster, the TICKING becoming
unbearable.

                              JON (V.O.)
                    I think of our friends. So many. I
                    think of their funerals.

                                             FLASH TO:

INT. HOSPITAL - NIGHT - FLASHBACK - 1990

As Jon sits in the hallway, two MEN (20s) stand outside of a
hospital room, one of them trying to comfort the other, who is
weeping uncontrollably.

                    JON (V.O.)
          I think of their parents, not even
          fifty, saying the Kaddish over their
          children.

                    MICHAEL (V.O.)
          IS THIS REAL LIFE?
          IS THIS REAL LIFE?

EXT. CENTRAL PARK - EVENING - 1990

Jon walks faster and faster.

                    JON (V.O.)
          I think of them and I think of Michael
          and, before I understand what's
          happening, I start running...

Jon breaks into a run, the Park nearly empty now.

EXT. GREAT LAWN - MINUTES LATER - 1990

Jon reaches the Great Lawn, still at a run.

          JON (V.O.)   MICHAEL (V.O.)
Past the pond, past the   IS THIS REAL LIFE?
Carousel...

The TICKING grows faster and louder, relentless, implacable, as
Jon runs through the vast, empty field, tears streaming down
his face, Michael's singing constant now.

          JON (V.O.)   MICHAEL (V.O.)
The ticking is so loud now, I   IS THIS REAL LIFE?
can't hear anything. My   IS THIS REAL
heartbeat is pounding in my   IS THIS REAL
throat. The wind is shrieking   IS THIS REAL
through the trees. The sky is   IS THIS REAL
darkening. I want it to stop. I
want it all to stop.

Jon suddenly sees something out of the corner of his eye. He
stops. The singing stops.

Dozens of SEAGULLS perch on a nearby hill, seemingly watching
him. He stands there, looking at them.

The birds take to the air en masse, flying away. Jon follows the birds with his eyes -- to the Delacorte, an exquisite outdoor theater, a hundred yards away.

EXT. CENTRAL PARK - MINUTES LATER - NIGHT - 1990

Jon stands outside the theater, the TICKING unabated. He peers in through the chain-link fence and sees a rehearsal piano, covered by a tarp. He begins to climb the fence.

EXT. DELACORTE THEATER - MOMENTS LATER - 1990

Jon looks around, sees that he is alone. He delicately pulls the tarp from the piano. He sits at the bench and puts his hands over the keys. All at once, the TICKING stops. The only thing he can hear is the sound of his own breathing. He begins to play **WHY**, tentatively at first, passion and intensity building with the song.

                    JON
          WHEN I WAS NINE,
          MICHAEL AND I
          ENTERED A TALENT SHOW DOWN AT THE Y

As Jon sings, we begin to INTERCUT with flashes to the past that he is remembering --

INT. YMCA BACKSTAGE AREA - DAY - FLASHBACK - 1969

YOUNG JON and YOUNG MICHAEL (both 9) practice a silly talent show number. Other KIDS practice nearby, a TEACHER supervising.

                    JON (V.O.)
          NINE A.M. WENT TO REHEARSE BY SOME
          STAIRS
          MIKE COULDN'T SING
          BUT I SAID, "NO ONE CARES"
          WE SANG "YELLOW BIRD" AND "LET'S GO
          FLY A KITE"
          OVER AND OVER AND OVER
          TILL WE GOT IT RIGHT

INT. YMCA STAGE - DAY - FLASHBACK - 1969

Young Jon and Young Michael bow with the other Kids.

                    JON (V.O.)
          WHEN WE EMERGED FROM THE YMCA
          THREE O'CLOCK SUN HAD MADE THE GRASS
          HAY
          I THOUGHT,
          HEY, WHAT A WAY TO SPEND A DAY
          HEY, WHAT A WAY TO SPEND A DAY
                    (MORE)

> JON (V.O.) (CONT'D)
> I MAKE A VOW, RIGHT HERE AND NOW
> I'M GONNA SPEND MY TIME THIS WAY

INT. DELACORTE THEATER - NIGHT - 1990

Jon plays the piano.

> JON
> WHEN I WAS SIXTEEN,
> MICHAEL AND I
> GOT PARTS IN *WEST SIDE*
> AT WHITE PLAINS HIGH

INT. HIGH SCHOOL GYM - DAY - FLASHBACK - 1976

TEENAGE JON and TEENAGE MICHAEL (both 16) rehearse *West Side Story* in costume with a group of fellow HIGH SCHOOLERS. Everyone is incredibly focused, earnest, and committed.

> JON
> THREE O'CLOCK WENT TO REHEARSE IN THE
> GYM
> MIKE PLAYED "DOC," WHO DIDN'T SING --
> FINE WITH HIM
> WE SANG "GOTTA ROCKET IN YOUR POCKET"
> AND "THE JETS ARE GONNA HAVE THEIR
> DAY, TONIGHT"
> OVER AND OVER AND OVER
> TILL WE GOT IT RIGHT

EXT. DELACORTE THEATER - NIGHT - 1990

Jon at the piano.

> JON
> WHEN WE EMERGED,
> WIPED OUT BY THAT PLAY
> NINE O'CLOCK, STARS AND MOON LIT THE
> WAY

INT. HIGH SCHOOL GYM - DAY - FLASHBACK - 1976

Teenage Jon and Teenage Michael join the rest of the company in rehearsing the curtain call.

> JON
> I THOUGHT,
> HEY, WHAT A WAY TO SPEND A DAY
> HEY, WHAT A WAY TO SPEND A DAY

EXT. DELACORTE THEATER - NIGHT - 1990

Jon at the piano.

                         JON
          I MADE A VOW, I WONDER NOW
          AM I CUT OUT TO SPEND MY TIME THIS
          WAY?
          WITH ONLY SO MUCH TIME TO SPEND
          DON'T WANNA WASTE THE TIME I'M GIVEN
          "HAVE IT ALL, PLAY THE GAME" -- SOME
          RECOMMEND
          I'M AFRAID, IT JUST MAY BE TIME TO
          GIVE IN
          I'M TWENTY-NINE, MICHAEL AND I
          LIVE ON THE WEST SIDE OF SOHO, NY
          NINE A.M., I WRITE A LYRIC OR TWO
          MIKE SINGS HIS SONG NOW ON MAD AVENUE
          I SING, "COME TO YOUR SENSES,
          DEFENSES ARE NOT THE WAY TO GO"
          OVER AND OVER AND OVER AND OVER AND
          OVER AND OVER AND OVER TILL I GET IT
          RIGHT
          WHEN I EMERGE FROM B MINOR OR A
          FIVE O'CLOCK, DINER CALLS, "I'M ON MY
          WAY"
          HEY, WHAT A WAY TO SPEND A DAY
          HEY, WHAT A WAY TO SPEND A DAY
          I MAKE A VOW - RIGHT HERE AND NOW
          I'M GONNA SPEND MY TIME THIS WAY
          I'M GONNA SPEND MY TIME THIS WAY

As Jon finishes, the skies open and it begins to pour.

INT. MICHAEL'S APARTMENT - NIGHT - 1990

Michael opens the door to find Jon standing there, soaking wet.

                         JON
          Whatever comes next... I'm here. I
          promise. There's a support group, it's
          called Friends In Deed. I just called
          them. They have a meeting tomorrow
          morning --

                         MICHAEL
          You look like shit.

                         JON
             (admitting)
          I'm so cold.

                         MICHAEL
             (laughs, opens door)
          Come on.

Jon steps forward, folding his arms around him. They stand
there, in the doorway, holding one another.

INT. THEATER - NIGHT - 1992

Jon at the piano.

> JON
> Sunday night. My thirtieth birthday.

INT. JON'S APARTMENT - NIGHT - 1990

Jon, kneeling on the living room floor, arranges dozens of pieces of paper. It's unclear exactly what they are. The phone RINGS. The outgoing MESSAGE sounds.

> JON (V.O.)
> *Speak.*

> SONDHEIM (V.O.)
> Jon? Steve Sondheim here. Rosa gave me
> this number. I hope it's okay to call
> you...
> (Jon freezes, stunned)
> I didn't get a chance to speak with
> you after your reading, but I just
> wanted to say it was really good.
> Congratulations. I'd love to get
> together and talk to you about it, if
> you have any interest. No pressure.

Jon laughs -- as if he might not have interest in that.

> SONDHEIM (V.O.)
> The main thing, though, is that it's
> first-rate work and it has a future.
> And so do you. I'll call you later
> with some thoughts if that's okay.
> Meanwhile, be proud.

As Jon turns to go, we see that the papers on the floor are a dozen pages torn out from his small spiral notebook -- filled with questions: "Fear or love?" "Why do we follow leaders that don't lead?" Etc.

INT. MOONDANCE DINER - NIGHT - 1990

A CLOSED sign hangs on the door of the Moondance, filled with a dozen or so FRIENDS of Jon's. Jon huddles with Carolyn.

> CAROLYN
> There was a small, very, very small,
> part of me that was... the teensiest
> bit happy to hear you're not leaving.

                    JON
          Well, I would have been sad not to see
          you every Sunday morning.

                    CAROLYN
          I told Freddy. He's pissed off at your
          agent.

                    JON
          How is he?

                    CAROLYN
          He should be going home soon.

Jon looks to the locked front door, sees Susan there. She
offers a smile. He returns it.

EXT. MOONDANCE DINER - MOMENTS LATER - 1990

Jon unlocks the door and joins Susan outside.

                    JON
          I didn't know that you were --

                    SUSAN
          I wasn't sure whether you would want
          me here.

                    JON
          I'm happy you came.

                    SUSAN
          How was the reading?

                    SUSAN (CONT'D)
          Did anyone...?

He shakes his head.

                    SUSAN (CONT'D)
          I'm sorry.

He shrugs -- what can you do?

                    SUSAN (CONT'D)
          I wanted to be there, I just...

                    JON
          I know.

                    SUSAN
          What are you going to do now?

                    JON
        Start the next one, I guess.

                    SUSAN
            (a beat)
        I decided to take the job.

                    JON
        I'm happy for you.

A long beat. Before it can get emotional, she hands him a
present.

                    SUSAN
        Happy Birthday.

He looks at it -- the beautiful book of manuscript paper he
wanted to buy at the Strand days earlier. She smiles.

                    SUSAN (CONT'D)
        For the next one. Do you have any
        ideas?

                    JON
            (shakes his head)
        Just questions.

                    SUSAN
        That seems like a really good place to
        start.
            (then)
        Goodbye, Jonathan.

Susan turns and goes. Jon stands there, looking after her. As
he does, we hear her VOICE.

                    SUSAN (V.O.)
        The next one was *tick, tick...boom!*
        After that, he went back to a project
        he'd started and put away, called
        Rent. It ran on Broadway for twelve
        years. It changed the definition of
        what a musical could be. What it could
        sound like. The kinds of stories that
        it could tell. Jonathan never got to
        see it. The night of the show's final
        dress rehearsal, he died from a sudden
        aortic aneurysm. He was thirty-five
        years old...

EXT. NEW YORK THEATER WORKSHOP - NIGHT - 1992

Before the show. Some last-minute STRAGGLERS make their way
into the theater.

As we follow them in, we linger on a flyer Scotch-taped there:
"tick, tick...BOOM! A rock monologue by Jonathan Larson.
December 14, 1992. One night-only."

                         SUSAN (V.O.)
              He still had so many questions.

INT. THEATER - NIGHT - 1992

Jon begins to play **LOUDER THAN WORDS** at the piano. Over the
course of the song we see his audience for the first time.

                         JON
              WHY DO WE PLAY WITH FIRE?
              WHY DO WE RUN OUR FINGER THROUGH THE
              FLAME?
              WHY DO WE LEAVE OUR HAND ON THE STOVE,
              ALTHOUGH WE KNOW, WE'RE IN FOR SOME
              PAIN?
              OH, WHY DO WE REFUSE TO HANG A LIGHT,
              WHEN THE STREETS ARE DANGEROUS?
              WHY DOES IT TAKE AN ACCIDENT,
              BEFORE THE TRUTH GETS THROUGH TO US?
              CAGES OR WINGS,
              WHICH DO YOU PREFER?
              ASK THE BIRDS
              FEAR OR LOVE, BABY
              DON'T SAY THE ANSWER
              ACTIONS SPEAK LOUDER THAN WORDS
              WHY SHOULD WE TRY TO BE OUR BEST
              WHEN WE CAN JUST GET BY AND STILL
              GAIN?
              WHY DO WE NOD OUR HEADS

                         JON AND ROGER
              ALTHOUGH WE KNOW

                         ROGER
              THE BOSS IS WRONG AS RAIN?

Jon looks out past the lights and sees Judy, the leader of the
focus group, vibing to the music next to former madrigals
singer Scott.

                         JON
              WHY SHOULD WE BLAZE A TRAIL
              WHEN THE WELL WORN PATH SEEMS SAFE AND

Jon sees Ira Weitzman.

                         JON AND KARESSA
              SO INVITING?

Jon sees Al and Nan, holding hands, bursting with pride.

                    KARESSA
          HOW, AS WE TRAVEL, CAN WE --

                JON AND KARESSA
          -- SEE THE DISMAY
          AND KEEP FROM FIGHTING?

          JON   ROGER AND KARESSA
CAGES OR WINGS   CAGES OR WINGS
WHICH DO YOU PREFER?   AH
ASK THE BIRDS

Jon sees Michael, almost as proud as his parents, healthy,
well, holding hands with DAVID (30s), his boyfriend.

                JON, ROGER, AND KARESSA
          FEAR OR LOVE, BABY
          DON'T SAY THE ANSWER

          JON   ROGER AND KARESSA
ACTIONS SPEAK LOUDER THAN WORDS   LOUDER THAN, LOUDER THAN

We see more of the audience. Freddy. Carolyn. Stephen Sondheim.
Cristin, Gerard, Danya, and Lauren from the *Superbia* workshop.
Even Rosa is there.

                JON (CONT'D)
          WHAT DOES IT TAKE
          TO WAKE UP A GENERATION?

                JON, ROGER, AND KARESSA
          HOW CAN YOU MAKE SOMEONE
          TAKE OFF AND FLY?

                JON
          IF WE DON'T WAKE UP
          AND SHAKE UP THE NATION
          WE'LL EAT THE DUST
          OF THE WORLD WONDERING

          JON (CONT'D)   ROGER AND KARESSA
WHY   WHY

Jon looks out, finds a sign on an empty seat: "Reserved for
Susan Wilson." She isn't coming. He takes this in.

                    KARESSA
          WHY DO WE STAY WITH LOVERS
          WHO WE KNOW, DOWN DEEP
          JUST AREN'T RIGHT?
          WHY WOULD WE RATHER

                        JON, ROGER, AND KARESSA
              PUT OURSELVES THROUGH HELL
              THAN SLEEP ALONE AT NIGHT?

                        JON
              WHY DO WE FOLLOW LEADERS WHO NEVER
              LEAD?

                        ROGER
              WHY DOES IT TAKE CATASTROPHE TO START
              A REVOLUTION

                        ROGER AND KARESSA
              IF WE'RE SO FREE
              TELL ME WHY

                        JON
              SOMEONE TELL ME WHY
              SO MANY PEOPLE BLEED

              JON (CONT'D)   ROGER AND KARESSA
CAGES OR WINGS   CAGES OR WINGS
WHICH DO YOU PREFER?   AH
ASK THE BIRDS

                        JON, ROGER, AND KARESSA
              FEAR OR LOVE, BABY
              DON'T SAY THE ANSWER

              JON   ROGER AND KARESSA
ACTIONS SPEAK LOUDER THAN WORDS   LOUDER THAN, LOUDER THAN,
                                   LOUDER THAN, LOUDER THAN

The band CUTS OUT and Jon, Roger, and Karessa sing a cappella.

                        ALL
              CAGES OR WINGS
              WHICH DO YOU PREFER?

                        JON
              ASK THE BIRDS

In the very back of the theater, unseen by Jon, Susan stands,
watching, rapt, feeling a million different things at once.

                        ALL
              AH
              FEAR OR LOVE, BABY
              DON'T SAY THE ANSWER

                        JON
              ACTIONS SPEAK LOUDER

                              ALL
              LOUDER THAN, LOUDER THAN, AH

                              JON
                    THEY SPEAK LOUDER

                              ALL
              LOUDER THAN, LOUDER THAN, AH

                              JON
                  ACTIONS SPEAK LOUDER THAN

INT. DINER - LATER - 1990

The LIGHTS go out. Jon stands in the center of the room, as
Michael comes, bearing a beautiful birthday cake. Donna stands,
her VHS camcorder pointed at Jon.

INT. THEATER - NIGHT - 1992

Jon plays a very simple, one-handed rendition of "Happy
Birthday" on the piano.

INT. DINER - MOMENTS LATER - 1990

Michael and the cake are right before Jon's eyes.

INT. THEATER - NIGHT - 1992

Jon finishes the melody on the piano, but omits the last note,
leaving the phrase unresolved.

INT. DINER - MOMENTS LATER - 1990

Silence. Michael smiles at Jon through the flickering of
birthday candles.

                         MICHAEL
                    Make a wish.

Jon considers for a moment. He inhales as we --

                                        SMASH TO BLACK.

                        THE END

Made in United States
Orlando, FL
26 June 2022